The Ex-Offender's Quick Job Hunting Guide

Ron and Caryl Krannich, Ph.Ds

IMPACT PUBLICATIONS
Manassas Park, VA

Warning/Liability/Warranty: The authors and publisher have made every attempt to provide the reader with accurate, timely, and useful information for making smart choices. However, given the rapid changes taking place in today's economy and job market, some of our information will inevitably change. The information presented here is for reference purposes only. The authors and publisher make no claims that using this information will guarantee the reader a job or lead to successful re-entry. The authors and publisher shall not be liable for any losses or damages incurred in the process of following the advice in this book.

ISBN: 1-57023-250-4

Library of Congress: 2005933658

Publisher: For information on Impact Publications, including current and forthcoming publications, authors, press kits, online bookstore, newsletters, downloadable catalogs, and submission requirements, visit the left navigation bar on the front page of our main company website: www.impactpublications.com.

Publicity/Rights: For information on publicity, author interviews, and subsidiary rights, contact the Media Relations Department: Tel. 703-361-7300, Fax 703-335-9486, or email: info@impactpublications.com.

Sales/Distribution: All sales and distribution inquiries should be directed to the publisher: Sales Department, IMPACT PUBLICATIONS, 9104 Manassas Drive, Suite N, Manassas Park, VA 20111-5211, Tel. 703-361-7300, Fax 703-335-9486, or email: info@impactpublications.com.

Quantity Discounts and Customized Editions: We offer quantity discounts and customized editions on bulk purchases. Please review our discount schedule for this book on the inside back cover, at www.impactpublications.com, or by contacting the Special Sales Department, Tel. 703-361-0255.

Authors: Ron and Caryl Krannich, Ph.Ds, are two of America's leading career and travel writers who have authored more than 70 books, including such bestsellers as *The Ex-Offender's Job Hunting Guide*, *High Impact Resumes and Letters*, *Interview for Success*, *No One Will Hire Me!*, *Job Interview Tips for People With Not-So-Hot Backgrounds*, *Nail the Job Interview!*, *Nail the Resume!*, *Nail the Cover Letter!*, *America's Top Jobs for People Re-Entering the Workforce*, *America's Top 100 Jobs for People Without a Four-Your Degree*, *101 Secrets of Highly Effective Speakers*, and *Change Your Job, Change Your Life*. Specializing on ex-offender re-entry and employment resources as well as individuals in transition, they are available for consultation and special presentations. They can be contacted through the publisher: krannich@impactpublications.com.

Contents

1

Put the 10 Steps
Into Practice

THIS WORKBOOK IS DESIGNED TO PUT the 10 steps to job search success into practice as outlined in *The Ex-Offender's Job Hunting Guide* (Impact Publications, 2005). Examining each of these steps, it helps you put into action an effective job search plan. If you complete each of the tests and exercises according to our directions, you should be well prepared to find a job that's best suited to your particular interests, skills, and goals.

Key Principles of Success

Throughout this workbook we emphasize five important principles for achieving job search and re-entry success:

1. **You are responsible for your own employment fate.** While many people will assist you with your job search by giving you useful information, advice, and referrals, **you** are responsible for taking the necessary actions to land a job. Don't rationalize your current situation, lack of progress, or frustrations by blaming other people or believing that you are a victim. After all, you are where you are because of **choices** you made. And don't expect other people to find or give you a job. You have to earn a job by communicating your qualifications to prospective employers and receiving their trust.

2. **You must develop and maintain a positive attitude and keep motivated throughout your job search.** Finding a job can be an extremely frustrating experience filled with many disappointments. It also can be a very exciting experience in which you learn a great deal about yourself and others as well as land a job you really love. While you will encounter numerous disappointments, frustrations, and rejections along the road to finding a job,

accept these negatives as part of the process of finding a job. It's very easy to become depressed and thus lose the motivation to complete each of the 10 steps to job search success. Constantly check your **attitude** to make sure it's positive and pointed in the right direction. In the end, your attitude will be your most important asset in finding a job and making a successful transition.

3. **You must be honest with yourself and others.** Take a good look in the mirror. Who and what do you see? If you have a history of deception and excuses, it's time to come clean and face who you really are. Several of our self-assessment exercises in Chapters 4, 7, and 8 will give you important information about yourself. Once you discover the **truth about you** – who you really are – there's no need to deceive yourself and others. Indeed, one of the most valuable things you may learn in this workbook is the truth about you and how to tell that truth to prospective employers who may want to hire you in spite of red flags in your background.

4. **You should disclose your record at the appropriate time and place.** When and to whom should you disclose your record? Given today's high-tech society, in which employers can easily conduct background checks, there's no place for ex-offenders to hide. The most appropriate time and place to disclose your record is **during a job interview** and before accepting a job offer. Many employers will ask about red flags in your background during a job interview or will conduct a background check just before or immediately after offering you a job. You should never disclose your criminal background in a letter or on a resume. This is an important issue that needs to be properly dealt with in a face-to-face meeting with a prospective employer.

5. **You must reach out to others who can assist you at various stages of your job search.** In addition to your attitude (Step 1 in Chapter 4), one of your most important re-entry assets will be your **support network** (Step 2 in Chapter 5) This includes family, friends, acquaintances, and organizations designed to assist ex-offenders. It involves the process of networking (Step 8 in Chapter 11). Make sure you develop a support network that can constantly give you information, advice, and referrals. Most important, your support network will give you encouragement and help you through the many psychological ups and downs of making a transition to the free world.

The 10 Steps to Job Search Success

The diagram on page 3 illustrates the 10 steps to job search success. Each step needs to be completed in the order outlined in this diagram.

Unfortunately, many job seekers fail to understand each of these steps and how they relate to one another. They often tend to start their job search with Step 7 – write resumes and letters – before knowing what they want to do (Step 5) or knowing what they do well and enjoy doing (Step 4). As a result, they tend to write awful resumes and letters that present a very weak picture of what they have done, can do, and will do in the future. In addition, their job search lacks a sense of purpose and direction. Such job seekers also tend to encounter numerous rejections because they simply don't know how to conduct an effective job search involving all of the 10 steps in their proper order.

10 Steps to Job Search Success

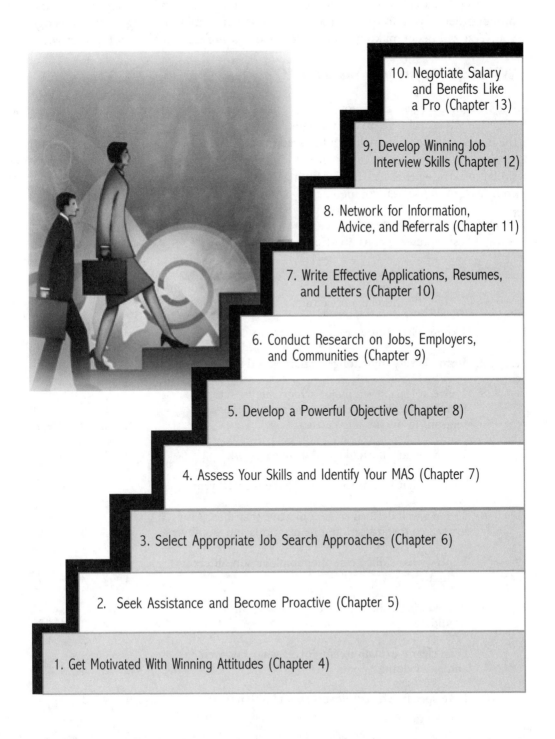

10. Negotiate Salary
and Benefits Like
a Pro (Chapter 13)

9. Develop Winning Job
Interview Skills (Chapter 12)

8. Network for Information,
Advice, and Referrals (Chapter 11)

7. Write Effective Applications, Resumes,
and Letters (Chapter 10)

6. Conduct Research on Jobs, Employers,
and Communities (Chapter 9)

5. Develop a Powerful Objective (Chapter 8)

4. Assess Your Skills and Identify Your MAS (Chapter 7)

3. Select Appropriate Job Search Approaches (Chapter 6)

2. Seek Assistance and Become Proactive (Chapter 5)

1. Get Motivated With Winning Attitudes (Chapter 4)

Take, for example, Step 1, "Get Motivated With Winning Attitudes." This is a foundation step for the remaining nine steps. Without the proper attitudes, which also affect your motivation and point you in the right direction, you will have difficulty completing the remaining steps. Step 4, "Assess Your Skills and Identify Your MAS," is one of the most important steps for completing Steps 5 through 10.

We strongly recommend that you frequently refer to the diagram on page 3 throughout your job search. Be sure to take the time to complete each step thoroughly and in the proper order. If you do this, you will be well on your way to finding a job that is right for you. You will begin making critical choices that will result in the right job for you.

What Is Your Job Search IQ?

Let's begin by examining how well prepared you are to organize and implement an effective job search. There are no right or wrong answers to the following quiz. Most of the issues included here will be addressed in each of the 10 steps. The exercise is designed to give you useful feedback by measuring your current level of job search information, skills, and strategies as well as identifying those you need to develop and improve. Identify your level of job search competence by completing the following exercise:

INSTRUCTIONS: Respond to each statement by circling which number at the right best represents your situation.

SCALE: 1 = Strongly agree   4 = Disagree
2 = Agree   5 = Strongly disagree
3 = Maybe, not certain

1. I know what motivates me to excel at work.	1 2 3 4 5
2. I can identify my strongest abilities and skills.	1 2 3 4 5
3. I have at least seven major achievements that reveal a pattern of interests and abilities that are relevant to my job and career.	1 2 3 4 5
4. I know what I both like and dislike in work.	1 2 3 4 5
5. I know what I want to do during the next 10 years.	1 2 3 4 5
6. I have a well defined career objective that directs my job search toward certain organizations and employers.	1 2 3 4 5
7. I know what skills I can offer employers in different occupations.	1 2 3 4 5
8. I know what skills employers most seek in candidates.	1 2 3 4 5
9. I can clearly explain to employers what I do well and enjoy doing.	1 2 3 4 5
10. I can specify why employers should hire me.	1 2 3 4 5

11. I can gain the support of family and friends
for making a job or career change.   1 2 3 4 5

12. I can find 10 to 20 hours a week to conduct
a job search.   1 2 3 4 5

13. I have the financial ability to conduct a job search
for up to three months.   1 2 3 4 5

14. I can conduct library and Internet research on
different occupations, employers, organizations,
and communities.   1 2 3 4 5

15. I can write different types of effective resumes
and job search/thank you letters.   1 2 3 4 5

16. I can produce and distribute resumes and letters
to the right people.   1 2 3 4 5

17. I can list my major accomplishments.   1 2 3 4 5

18. I can identify and target employers I want to
interview.   1 2 3 4 5

19. I know how to use the Internet to conduct
employment research and network.   1 2 3 4 5

20. I know which websites are best for posting my
resumes and browsing job postings.   1 2 3 4 5

21. I know how much time I should spend conducting
an online job search.   1 2 3 4 5

22. I can develop a job referral network.   1 2 3 4 5

23. I can persuade others to join in forming a job
search support group.   1 2 3 4 5

24. I can look for job leads.   1 2 3 4 5

25. I can use the telephone to develop prospects and
get referrals and interviews.   1 2 3 4 5

26. I can plan and implement an effective direct-mail
job search campaign.   1 2 3 4 5

27. I can persuade employers to interview me.   1 2 3 4 5

28 I have a list of at least 10 questions about the
company I need to ask during interviews.   1 2 3 4 5

29. I know the best time to talk about salary with an
employer.   1 2 3 4 5

30. I know what I want to do with my life over
    the next 10 years.   1   2   3   4   5

31. I have a clear pattern of accomplishments which
    I can explain to employers, giving examples.   1   2   3   4   5

32. I have little difficulty in making cold calls and
    striking up conversations with strangers.   1   2   3   4   5

33. I usually take responsibility for my own actions
    rather than blame other people for my situation
    or circumstance.   1   2   3   4   5

34. I can generate at least one job interview for every
    10 job search contacts I make.   1   2   3   4   5

35. I can follow up on job interviews.   1   2   3   4   5

36. I can negotiate a salary 10-20% above what an
    employer initially offers.   1   2   3   4   5

37. I can persuade an employer to renegotiate my
    salary after six months on the job.   1   2   3   4   5

38. I can create a position for myself in an organization.   1   2   3   4   5

TOTAL

Calculate your potential job search effectiveness by adding the numbers you circled for an overall score. If your total is more than 90 points, you need to work on developing your job search. How you scored each item will indicate to what degree you need to work on improving specific job search skills, which we will examine in the remaining chapters of this workbook. If your score is under 60 points, you are well on your way toward job search success!

2

Focus On Important Questions, Answers, and Exercises

STARTING A NEW LIFE IN THE WORLD of work begins with a series of carefully crafted questions related to your interests, skills, and goals. These questions are the basis for developing a step-by-step approach to making a successful transition to the free world.

The old adage that half of the solution to any problem begins with the **question** is especially true when looking for a job. While we are often preoccupied with finding answers, we seldom look at the **quality of our questions**. If, for example, you ask the wrong question, you are likely to get an answer that will lead to an unhappy outcome. Indeed, the particular questions we ask may prove to be more important than the specific answers to questions. If you ask the right questions, you'll get the right answers.

Throughout this workbook, we have attempted to focus on high quality questions that will yield the most useful answers to making a transition to the world of work. These questions, in turn, are related to a series of practical exercises that generate usable information for finding a job. Take, for example, the following question job seekers ask:

How do I write a resume?

While this is an important question, it should only be asked **after** other more important questions have been raised about your interests, skills, accomplishments, and goals:

- *What do you do especially well?*
- *What do you enjoy doing?*
- *What are your major accomplishments?*
- *What do you want to be doing over the next five years?*

Once you have answered these questions by completing a series of exercises, you then are prepared to address other important questions:

- *What type of resume should I write?*
- *Who will I send it to?*
- *How should I send it?*

Once you have answered all of these questions, then you will be prepared to address what may now seem to be a relatively insignificant question: *How do I write a resume?* In other words, you need to ask the **right questions** at the right time. In so doing, the answers will be readily forthcoming.

Let's take another question often asked by ex-offenders:

Where can I find a job in construction?

This question is often asked by individuals who think the most important thing they need to know about finding a job is **where** to locate a specific job. By asking this question, you have either answered many more important questions or you have prematurely asked a question that is likely to yield some unsatisfactory and disappointing answers. In other words, this may be an inappropriate question to ask at this stage of your job search. The answer to this question becomes self-evident once you address a series of other questions that will prove to be more useful for your job search. Most of these are self-assessment questions that yield a great deal of useful information about how you can best relate to the world of work:

- *What am I most interested in doing?*
- *What are my major strengths that would appeal to employers?*
- *How do my skills relate to specific occupational fields and jobs?*
- *What types of jobs am I most qualified to perform?*
- *What type of construction job would I be best at doing?*

Let's begin with an exercise that focuses on the quality of your questions. List the five most important questions you seek answers to for finding a job:

1. _____

2. _____

3. _____

4. _____

5. _____

Now, restate each of your questions two different ways and then circle one that is most likely to give you the most useful information for finding a job:

Question 1: _____

1a _____

1b _____

Question 2: _____

2a _____

2b _____

Question 3: _____

3a _____

3b _____

Question 4: _____

4a _____

4b _____

Question 5: _____

5a _____

5b _____

Now restate the five most important questions you seek answers to for finding a job:

1. _____

2. _____

3. _____

4. _____

5. _____

3

Take Responsibility and Tell the Truth

THREE OF THE MOST CHALLENGING aspects of re-entry are (1) taking responsibility for your past, (2) telling the truth about your background to prospective employers, and (3) building trust between you and others. Since you are responsible for shaping your future, you must begin by being truthful to yourself by taking responsibility for your actions. Only then can you begin building the necessary **trust** that is so important for developing and maintaining long-term supportive relationships.

Taking Responsibility for Your Choices

The first step to changing your life is to admit responsibility for your own situation. Life doesn't just happen or fall out of the sky. You make **choices** that have consequences. Some people make lots of bad choices that result in difficult situations. Let's look at some of your choices and their consequences. What five bad and five good choices have you made during the past 10 years? What happened as a result of those choices?

Bad Choices	Consequences/Results
_____	_____
_____	_____
_____	_____
_____	_____
_____	_____

Good Choices	**Consequences/Results**
_____	_____
_____	_____
_____	_____
_____	_____
_____	_____

Once you take responsibility for your choices, you can begin discarding some baggage that otherwise may continue to weigh you down. Since you have the power within you to change your life, you need to become better acquainted with your ability to create your future. It won't be easy, but nothing worthwhile is ever easy. You have to work at it day after day until your new attitudes and actions become positive and productive behaviors.

Maybe you've had bad luck, but so have many other successful people. Start by asking yourself these questions:

- Do you have dreams that motivate you to do your very best?

- Do you run with winners or hang around losers?

- What have you done to change your luck?

- Do you have goals and a detailed plan of action for taking charge of your life?

- How many people have you truthfully told your story to and asked for their advice on how you can change your life?

- When tomorrow comes, what five things do you have on a "To Do" list that will help you get ahead?

- Will you develop a new relationship with a person who can assist you?

- Will you take advantage of education and training opportunities?

- Will you visit your local library or One-Stop Career Center (see pages 33-34) to learn something new about jobs and employers?

- Will you call several employers to see if they have job opportunities?

- Have you used to your best ability both pre- and post-release re-entry resources, from educational programs to your probation or parole officer?

The point here is very simple: If you do nothing to get ahead, you'll get nothing in return. Indeed, people who don't take responsibility for themselves and their choices most likely become a victim of circumstances. You need to develop a positive and proactive attitude that constantly puts you in new places and with new people who can assist you.

Telling the Truth – Who Are You?

Few people are good at talking about themselves. Indeed, they are more comfortable talking about others than discussing their own strengths and weaknesses. Nonetheless, you will need to talk about yourself to employers who are interested in learning about your background, interests, skills, goals, ability to perform a job, and your trustworthiness.

One of the first and most important questions employers ask candidates is one you need to constantly ask yourself **before** entering the job market:

Tell me about yourself.

This is a very wide open question that can be answered many different ways. Since employers need to "read between the lines" for clues about strangers they could possibly hire, how you answer this question can be very revealing of your background, motivation, and behaviors. Here are some alternative ways of responding to this statement:

1. **Reveal the frank truth about yourself.** Tell the whole truth, including many negative things about your background, which includes your criminal background and incarceration.

2. **Tell the big lie.** Make up a nice story, however false, that will impress the listener.

3. **Avoid the issue.** Avoid volunteering information and talking about yourself by redirecting the question:

   "There's not much I can tell you."

   "Could we come back to that later?"

   "Is there anything in particular you would like to know?"

4. **Focus only on personal milestones and statistics.** Reveal date and place of birth, educational background, marital status, health, and names of previous employers.

5. **Emphasize key skills and accomplishments.** Talk about those things of most interest to the employer – what you can do for him or her in the future.

The first four responses to this are problematic. Indeed, many candidates choose the first response and thus ramble on about their backgrounds. Most of what they have to say is of little interest to employers, except when they volunteer their weaknesses or negatives. When they do this, they raise red flags that can knock them out of the competition. Many ex-offenders wish to avoid this issue altogether, since they believe telling the truth may eliminate them from consideration for the job.

But what truth are you trying to tell an employer? Are you being unfair to both yourself and potential employers when you try to deal with the truth? Here's the truth about the truth. While employers want you to tell the truth, they do not need to hear your whole life history. Remember, they are interested in possibly hiring you. What is it they are hiring? Your background? An ex-offender? No, they are hiring your **skills** – those things you can do for them that produce positive outcomes for their company or organization. How you answer this and other important questions may reveal your attitudes, motivations, and goals that may or may not be compatible with those of the company. A more detailed examination of your skills and performance – based on background check, tests, and a situational interview (see Chapter 12) – should give the employer some idea as to how well you can and will actually do the job.

Assume you have just been invited to a job interview. After greeting the interviewer and engaging in a small talk to put each other at ease, the interviewer starts the interview with this classic beginning interview statement – *"Tell me about yourself."* What he or she is really asking is this two-part question:

- *What is it you can do for me?*
- *Why should I hire you?*

This opening statement and related questions may well be the most important part of the job interview. How you deal with them may well set the tone for the remainder of the interview and determine whether or not you will be offered the job. Since we know first impressions count the most, your response to this statement will give the interviewer one of the most important impressions of the interview. So take this opening statement very seriously and put your best foot forward in revealing the truth about you to the prospective employer.

Exercise: On three sheets of paper, write your response to an interviewer's opening statement:

Tell me about yourself.

Based on the five choices we outlined on page 12 for responding to this statement, write exactly what you would like to say about yourself to a prospective employer who basically knows nothing about you beyond the information you may have provided on an application or resume. Try to keep your response to two or three minutes. Do not ramble on for five to 10 minutes. Prospective employers are not impressed with candidates who talk too much. Indeed, the longer you talk, the more likely you will begin revealing weaknesses rather than continue to stress your strengths!

Once you have completed this exercise, share your answer with someone you trust to give you thoughtful feedback on the quality of your response. Ask them to assume the role of the interviewer:

- What impression does my response make on you?
- What additional questions does my response raise?
- On a scale of 1 to 10, with "10" representing an outstanding response, how would you rate my response?
- How could I best improve my response?

Red Flags in Your Background

We all have red flags in our backgrounds. What are yours? In addition to being incarcerated, perhaps you dropped out of school, failed an important test, lost a job, experienced financial difficulties, got divorced, became seriously ill, lack experience and goals, abused drugs or alcohol, don't relate well to others, have work-related problems and poor references, have a learning disorder or physical handicap, or are a job hopper with an unstable work history. Most red flags relate to health, legal, financial, personal, learning, and behavioral problems in your past. For employers, such red flags reveal potential on-the-job problems they would like to avoid. If you have many red flags in your background that are likely to become employment issues, you need to deal with these **before** they become potential knock-outs on resumes, in job interviews, or on the job.

If you have ever been fired for the following high-risk behaviors, you have red flags in your background which may knock you out of consideration for a job if the employer learns about them from your references or a background check:

- Absent and tardy
- Broke rules
- Insubordinate
- Lying
- Stealing
- Uncooperative
- Drug and alcohol abuse

- Fighting on the job
- Bad attitude
- Dishonest
- Incompetent
- Abuse co-workers or clients
- Unpredictable behavior
- Lazy and undependable

Respond to the following statements to determine how "not-so-hot" your background may be. Circle the numbers to the right of each statement that best represents your degree of agreement or disagreement:

1 = Strongly agree   4 = Disagree
2 = Agree   5 = Strongly disagree
3 = Uncertain

1.	I have little work experience.	1	2	3	4	5
2.	I have work experience, but it is doing very different work from what I want to do.	1	2	3	4	5
3.	My grades in school were not very good.	1	2	3	4	5
4.	I lack a high school diploma or GED.	1	2	3	4	5
5.	I did not go to college or I dropped out of college.	1	2	3	4	5
6.	I have been fired from one job.	1	2	3	4	5
7.	I have been fired from more than one job.	1	2	3	4	5
8.	I have held several jobs in the last three years.	1	2	3	4	5
9.	I don't have a past employer who would give me a good reference.	1	2	3	4	5

10. The jobs I have held have each been very different
    from each other in terms of the work to be done and
    skills required.   1   2   3   4   5

11. I have been convicted of a felony.   1   2   3   4   5

12. I have a learning disability.   1   2   3   4   5

13. I have difficulty relating to others.   1   2   3   4   5

14. I've experienced some major health problems.   1   2   3   4   5

15. I've experienced marital problems.   1   2   3   4   5

16. My financial situation is difficult.   1   2   3   4   5

17. I've abused drugs and/or alcohol.   1   2   3   4   5

18. I've experienced mental health problems.   1   2   3   4   5

19. I have an arrest record.   1   2   3   4   5

20. If an employer knew much about my employment
    background, I would probably not be hired.   1   2   3   4   5

21. If an employer knew much about my personal
    background, I would probably not be hired.   1   2   3   4   5

TOTAL

If you circled a "1" or "2" for any of these statements, you may raise a red flag in the eyes of most employers. If your total score is between 26 and 60, you will most likely appear to have a not-so-hot background in the eyes of most employers. You'll need to develop job search strategies to overcome your job market weaknesses.

The first thing you need to do in dealing with red flags is to identify and acknowledge them as potential job knock-outs. Denying them or making excuses will not help you take corrective actions that can make you more employable. Once you've identified your red flags, the next step is to develop strategies for turning red flags into green flags that tell employers that you will be a good hire. You can start this process by asking yourself the following questions:

1. What questions might an employer ask about my background that could raise red flags concerning my fitness for the job?

_____

_____

2   What five things about my background could knock me out of consideration for a job?

_____

_____

_____

_____

_____

3.   What potential red flag behaviors might I need to re-examine and take greater responsibility for in the future?

_____

_____

_____

4.   What positive actions have I taken to change the negative behaviors that raise red flags?

_____

_____

_____

5.   Why would someone want to hire me?

_____

_____

_____

6.   What are my best work characteristics?

_____

_____

_____

For more information on potential red flags affecting a job search and how to best deal with them, see Caryl and Ron Krannich, *Job Interview Tips for People With Not-So-Hot Backgrounds* (Impact Publications, 2004).

4

Get Motivated With Winning Attitudes

EW EX-OFFENDERS RE-ENTER SOCIETY with a positive, can-do attitude. Many feel worthless, hopeless, and unwanted. Their negative attitudes are often obvious to family, friends, and employers. Not surprisingly, those attitudes affect their motivation in finding a job. Some simply aren't motivated to succeed.

Your attitude may well become your most important asset for re-entry success. However, your re-entry will probably be filled with anxiety and uncertainty – uncertain how people will receive you, uncertain about your family, uncertain about your housing and financial situations, and uncertain whether or not you will find a job and succeed on the outside. If you harbor anger, express negative attitudes, and a lack a sense of responsibility, chances are you also don't have the necessary motivation to become successful. If you are an older ex-offender, who may have been incarcerated for several years, you may be especially fearful of re-entering the job market and society. Unlike many young offenders, older ex-offenders often lack self-motivation skills that are essential for success.

What's Your Attitude?

If you have nothing to start with, at least you have an attitude that will potentially motivate you and thus propel you to success. On the other hand, your attitude might drag you down a road to failure. Take a moment to examine your attitude. Is it negative much of the time? Do you often make excuses? Does your attitude show in what you say and do? Are others attracted to you in a positive manner? What motivates you to succeed?

One of the first things you need to do is check the state of your attitude. You can do this by completing the following exercise. Check whether or not you primarily agree ("Yes") or disagree ("No") with each of these statements:

	Yes	No
1. Other people often make my work and life difficult.	❏	❏
2. When I get into trouble, it's often because of what someone else did rather than my fault.	❏	❏
3. People often take advantage of me.	❏	❏
4. When I worked, people less qualified than me often got promoted.	❏	❏
5. I avoid taking risks because I'm afraid of failing.	❏	❏
6. I don't trust many people.	❏	❏
7. Not many people trust me.	❏	❏
8. Not many people I know take responsibility.	❏	❏
9. Most people get ahead because of connections, schmoozing, and politics.	❏	❏
10. When I worked, I was assigned more duties than other people in similar positions.	❏	❏
11. I expect to be discriminated against in the job search and on the job.	❏	❏
12. I don't feel like I can change many things; I've been dealt this hand, so I'll have to live with it.	❏	❏
13. I've had my share of bad luck.	❏	❏
14. I usually have to do things myself rather than rely on others to get things done.	❏	❏
15. People often pick on me.	❏	❏
16. Employers try to take advantage of job seekers by offering them low salaries.	❏	❏
17. I didn't like many of the people I worked with.	❏	❏
18. There's not much I can do to get ahead.	❏	❏
19. My ideas are not really taken seriously.	❏	❏
20. I often think of reasons why other people's ideas won't work.	❏	❏
21. Other people are often wrong but I have to put up with them nonetheless.	❏	❏

22. I sometimes respond to suggestions by saying *"Yes, but . . . ,"* *"I'm not sure . . . ," "I don't think it will work . . . ," "Let's not do that . . ."*   ❑   ❑

23. I don't see why I need to get more education and training.   ❑   ❑

24. I often wish other people would just disappear.   ❑   ❑

25. I sometimes feel depressed.   ❑   ❑

26. I have a hard time getting and staying motivated.   ❑   ❑

27. I don't look forward to going to work.   ❑   ❑

28. Friday is my favorite workday.   ❑   ❑

29. When I worked, I sometimes came to work late, left early, or missed work altogether.   ❑   ❑

30. The jobs I've had didn't reflect my true talents.   ❑   ❑

31. I should have advanced a lot further than where I am today.   ❑   ❑

32. I'm worth a lot more than most employers are willing to pay.   ❑   ❑

33. I've been known to do things behind my boss's back that could get me into trouble.   ❑   ❑

TOTALS   ____   ____

Not all of these statements necessarily reflect bad attitudes or negative behaviors. Some may accurately reflect realities you encounter. In fact, some organizations breed negative attitudes and behaviors among their employees. However, if you checked "Yes" to more than six of these statements, you may be harboring some bad attitudes that affect both your job search and your on-the-job performance. You may want to examine these attitudes as possible **barriers to getting ahead** in your job search as well as on the job. Indeed, you may want to change those attitudes that may be preventing you from making good choices and getting ahead.

Examples of Attitudes I Need to Change

1. _____

2. _____

3. _____

4. _____

5. _____

I Will Change These Attitudes By Doing the Following

_____

_____

_____

_____

_____

What Excuses Do You Make?

Many negative attitudes are related to excuses we make for our behavior. Take, for example, the following list of "100 Excuses for Choosing Poor Behavior" compiled by Rory Donaldson on www.brainsarefun.com. While many of these excuses apply to school children, many also relate to everyone else. He prefaces this list with Rudyard Kipling's observation that *"We have forty million reasons for failure, but not a single excuse"*:

1. It's your fault.
2. I'm not happy.
3. It's too hot.
4. I'm too busy.
5. I'm sad.
6. I didn't sleep well.
7. It's not fair.
8. I wanted to watch TV.
9. I didn't write it down.
10. It's too hard.
11. It's too far away.
12. The teacher didn't explain it.
13. I forgot.
14. The dog was sick.
15. There was too much traffic.
16. I tried.
17. My pencil broke.
18. My grandmother wouldn't let me.
19. You're mean.
20. I didn't know it was today.
21. I'm too tired.
22. My brother was sick.
23. The car broke down.
24. It was snowing.
25. I hurt my foot.
26. I thought it was due tomorrow.
27. The ice was too thin.
28. I ran out of time.
29. I hurt my finger.
30. I don't feel well.
31. You didn't tell me.
32. It was cold.
33. I'm not good at that.
34. I left it in my pocket.
35. He made a face at me.
36. I wasn't.
37. I was rushed.
38. You didn't give it to me.
39. We did that last year.
40. That's not the way we learned at school.
41. His mother said it was O.K.
42. I already did it.
43. It was right here.
44. It's too much work.
45. It stinks.
46. I didn't know it was sharp.
47. I was scared.
48. I was frustrated.
49. I did it already.
50. It wasn't in the dictionary.
51. I lost it.
52. Nobody likes me.
53. I have poor self esteem.
54. I'm too happy.
55. I'm sleepy.
56. He hit me.
57. I already know that.
58. I left it at school.
59. It's too easy.
60. It's not important.
61. I couldn't get into my locker.
62. I dropped it.
63. I have a learning disorder.
64. I lost my pencil.
65. My pen leaked.

66. I have an excuse.
67. It got wet.
68. It got dirty.
69. My dog threw up.
70. I missed the bus.
71. I have a different learning style.
72. It was raining.
73. My grandfather was visiting.
74. I didn't know.
75. No one told me.
76. I don't have to.
77. My neck hurts.
78. I ran out of paper.
79. The electricity went out.
80. I don't know how.
81. I can't.
82. I don't know where it is.
83. He hit me first.
84. It's the weekend.
85. I ran out of money.
86. I'm too stupid.
87. My teacher said to do it this way.
88. I watched it at my friend's house.
89. I just cleaned it.
90. My friend got one.
91. You lost it.
92. It takes too much time.
93. He told me I didn't have to.
94. I'm hungry.
95. I couldn't open the door.
96. I'm too important.
97. It spilled.
98. I ran out of batteries.
99. I'm doing something else.
100. I didn't know it was hot.

We and other employers have often encountered 21 additional excuses related to the workplace. Some are even used by candidates during a job interview to explain their on-the-job behavior! Most of these excuses reflect an attitude lacking in responsibility and initiative:

1. No one told me.
2. I did what you said.
3. Your directions were bad.
4. It's not my fault.
5. She did it.
6. It just seemed to happen.
7. It happens a lot.
8. What did he say?
9. I had a headache.
10. I don't understand why.
11. I don't know how to do it.
12. That's your problem.
13. It wasn't very good.
14. Maybe you did it.
15. I thought I wrote it down.
16. That's not my style.
17. He told me to do it that way.
18. It's not my job.
19. I've got to go now.
20. Where do you think it went?
21. We can talk about it later.

We all make excuses. Many are harmless excuses that help us get through the day. Identify a few excuses you frequently make:

1. _____

2. _____

3. _____

4. _____

5. _____

On the other hand, certain excuses may prevent you from getting and keeping a job. Identify any excuses you make that may work against finding and keeping a job:

1. _____

2. _____

3. _____

4. _____

5. _____

When you express such excuses, you literally show an attitude that is not appreciated by employers. People with positive attitudes and proactive behavior do not engage in behaviors that reflect such excuses. They have a "can do" attitude that helps focus their minds on doing those things that are most important to achieving their goals. For example, rather than show up 10 minutes late for a job interview and say they got lost or had bad directions, people with positive attitudes and proactive behavior check out the interview location the day before in anticipation of arriving 10 minutes early. They make no excuses because they plan ahead and engage in no-excuses behavior!

Does Your Attitude Show?

The job search is all about making good first impressions on strangers who know little or nothing about your background and capabilities. Whether completing an application, writing a resume, or interviewing for a job, your attitude will show in many different ways, both verbally and nonverbally.

Many job seekers show attitudes of disrespect, deceit, laziness, irresponsibility, and carelessness – all red flags that will quickly eliminate you from the competition. Most of these attitudes are communicated during the critical job interview when employers have a chance to read both verbal and nonverbal behavioral cues. Here are some common mistakes job seekers make that show off some killer attitudes that also reflect on their character:

Mistake	Attitude/Character
▪ Lacks a job objective	Confused and unfocused
▪ Misspells words on application, resume, and letters	Careless and uneducated
▪ Uses poor grammar	Uneducated and illiterate
▪ Sends resume to the wrong person	Careless and error-prone
▪ Arrives late for the job interview	Unreliable and inconsiderate
▪ Dresses inappropriately	Unperceptive and insensitive
▪ Doesn't know about the company	Lazy and thoughtless
▪ Talks about salary and benefits	Greedy and self-centered
▪ Bad-mouths previous employer	Disrespectful and angry
▪ Doesn't admit to any weaknesses	Disingenuous and calculating
▪ Boasts about himself	Obnoxious and self-centered
▪ Lies about background	Deceitful
▪ Lacks eye contact	Shifty and dishonest
▪ Blames others for problems	Irresponsible
▪ Interrupts and argues	Inconsiderate and impatient

- Has trouble answering questions . . . . Unprepared and nervous
- Fails to ask any questions . . . . Uninterested in job
- Jumps from one extreme to another . . . . Manic and unfocused
- Fails to close and follow up interview . . . . Doesn't care about the job

On the other hand, employers look for attitudes that indicate a candidate has some of the following positive characteristics:

- Accurate
- Adaptable
- Careful
- Competent
- Considerate
- Cooperative
- Dependable
- Determined
- Diligent
- Discreet
- Educated
- Efficient
- Empathic
- Energetic
- Enthusiastic
- Fair
- Focused
- Good-natured
- Happy
- Helpful
- Honest
- Intelligent
- Loyal

- Nice
- Open-minded
- Patient
- Perceptive
- Precise
- Predictable
- Prompt
- Purposeful
- Reliable
- Resourceful
- Respectful
- Responsible
- Self-motivated
- Sensitive
- Sincere
- Skilled
- Tactful
- Team player
- Tenacious
- Tolerant
- Trustworthy
- Warm

Change Your Attitudes

If you have negative attitudes and often need to make excuses for your behavior, you are probably an unhappy person. It's time you took control of both your attitudes and behaviors. Start by identifying several of your negative attitudes and try to transform them into positive attitudes. As you do this, you will begin to identify the positive-minded person you want to be. For starters, examine these sets of negative and positive attitudes that can arise at various stages of the job search, especially during the critical job interview:

Negative Attitude	Positive Attitude
I've just got out of prison and need a job.	While incarcerated, I turned my life around by getting my GED, learning new skills, and controlling my anger. I'm really excited about becoming a landscape architect and working with your company.

I didn't like my last employer.	It was time for me to move on to a more progressive company.
I haven't been able to find a job in over three months. I really want this one.	I've been learning a great deal during the past several weeks of my job search.
My last two jobs were problems.	I learned a great deal about what I really love to do from those last two jobs.
Do you have a job for me?	I'm in the process of conducting a job search. Do you know anyone who might have an interest in someone with my qualifications?
I can't come in for an interview tomorrow since I'm interviewing for another job. What about Wednesday? That looks good.	I have a conflict tomorrow. Wednesday would be good. Could we do something in the morning?
Yes, I flunked out of college in my sophomore year.	After two years in college I decided to pursue a career in computer sales.
I really hated studying math.	Does this job require math?
Sorry about that spelling error on my resume. I was never good at spelling.	(Doesn't point it out; if the interviewer asked, replied *"It's one that got away."*)
I don't enjoy working in teams.	I work best when given an assignment that allows me to work on my own.
What does this job pay?	How does the pay scale here compare with other firms in the area?
Will I have to work weekends?	What are the normal hours for someone in this position?
I have to see my parole officer once a month. Can I have that day off?	I have an appointment I need to keep the last Friday of each month. Would it be okay if I took off three hours that day?
I'm three months pregnant. Will your health care program cover my delivery?	Could you tell me more about your benefits, such as health and dental care?

Can you think of any particular negative attitudes or situations you might have that you can restate in positive language? Identify five that relate to your job search and work. State them in both the negative and positive:

Negative Attitude/Situation   **Positive Attitude**

1. _____   _____

   _____   _____

   _____   _____

2. _____   _____

   _____   _____

   _____   _____

3. _____   _____

   _____   _____

   _____   _____

4. _____   _____

   _____   _____

   _____   _____

5. _____   _____

   _____   _____

   _____   _____

5

Seek Assistance and Become Proactive

WHO WILL HELP YOU WITH your re-entry, especially with finding a job? Will you be on your own or will you be working with various support groups? Whom will you initially look to for assistance in your community? Once you've been released, chances are you will return to your former community where you will seek employment along with food, housing, transportation, credit, health care, and other necessities of life. You will probably re-unite with many friends, relatives, and acquaintances, including former employers. If you are on parole or probation, the terms of your release may require that you become documented, live and work in one community, regularly see your P.O., disclose your criminal history to employers, and avoid certain jobs because of your background.

If you're lucky, you may be quickly hired by a former employer or land a job through a family connection or referral from a friend. In fact, these are the best sources for finding a job, regardless of your background – informal, word-of-mouth contacts that also screen you for employment and thus help you deal with the troubling issue of disclosure.

However, not everyone is fortunate to have great personal connections to quickly find a job. Many ex-offenders, who quickly exhaust their meager gate money, are in a scary survival mode – they need to get a job **now** just to pay for basic food, housing, and transportation.

The first thing you need to do is to understand various **community safety nets** designed to assist ex-offenders in transition. A community is more than just a place in which you live, work, and raise a family. A community also is a place of opportunities to fulfill your dreams. It's made up of many individuals, groups, organizations, institutions, and neighborhoods that come together for achieving different goals. They provide **opportunity structures** for finding jobs through informal, word-of-mouth channels. They become important **networks** for locating job opportunities. Some of these networks serve as safety networks, but most should be viewed as **networks of opportunity**. These are networks through which many good jobs may be found.

The larger the community, the more safety nets and opportunity networks will be available to you. For example, the safety nets for ex-offenders in Chicago, Houston, New York City, Baltimore, and Washington, DC are much greater than in Sioux Falls, South Dakota or Grand Prairie, Texas. However, the opportunity networks may be fewer in large poor cities that have high unemployment rates than in smaller cities and suburbs that have booming economies with very low unemployment.

Key Community Players for Ex-Offenders

Let's outline the key community players who can provide both a safety net and job opportunities for ex-offenders. They generally fall into these categories:

- **Government agencies and programs:** Social services, public health, courts, P.O.s, half-way houses, and One-Stop Career Centers.

- **Nonprofit and volunteer organizations:** Substance abuse centers, housing groups, public health groups, mental health organizations, legal services, and education and training organizations. Some of the most prominent such organizations that regularly work with ex-offenders include Goodwill Industries and the Salvation Army.

- **Churches and other faith-based organizations:** Includes a wide range of denominations that offer everything from evangelical to social services as well as faith-based organizations involved in the federal government's new Ready4Work Prisoner Reentry Initiative jointly funded by the U.S. Department of Labor (Center for Faith-Based and Community Initiatives), the U.S. Department of Justice, and a consortium of private foundations.

A good way to look at communities is to visualize the safety nets and opportunity networks relating to you as found in the diagram on page 28.

Let's take, for example, the City of Baltimore, Maryland. Each year nearly 9,000 ex-offenders are released into this city. Like ex-offenders in many other large cities, nearly 80 percent in Baltimore move into the worst neighborhoods. Recognizing that both the city and ex-offenders face a major challenge, Baltimore has been very aggressive in dealing with the problem of ex-offenders becoming re-offenders by pulling together major community resources for dealing with the re-entry issue. The Mayor's Office of Employment Development facilitated the creation of the Baltimore Citywide Ex-offender Task Force in October 2002 to focus on ex-offender re-entry issues (www.oedworks.com/exoffender. htm). The Task Force included more than 100 government agencies and community partners. In March 2004, the Task Force was succeeded by a Mayoral-appointed Ex-Offender Employment Steering Committee. Many of these agencies and organizations function as safety nets and opportunity networks for individuals who are unemployed, homeless, hungry, sick, victims of domestic violence, mentally ill, HIV/AIDS, or drug and alcohol abusers. Examples of such service providers include:

Community Safety Nets and Opportunity Networks

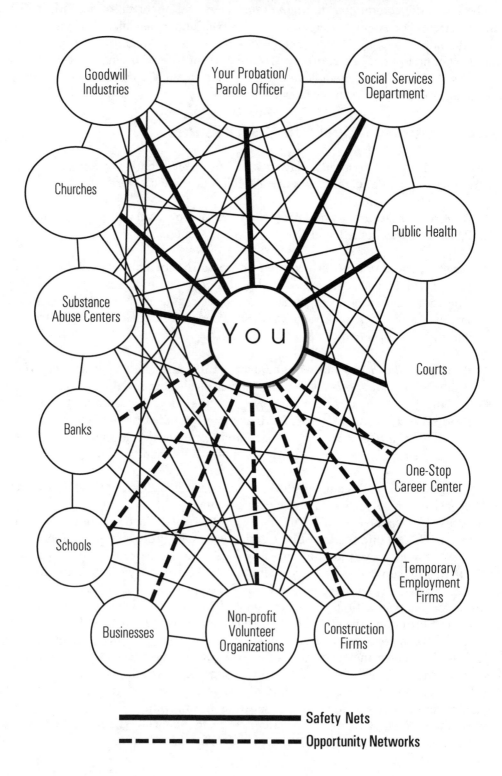

Employment

- Baltimore Works One-Stop Career Center
- Career Development and Cooperative Education Center
- Caroline Center
- Damascus Career Center
- Goodwill Industries of the Chesapeake
- Maryland New Directions
- Prisoners Aid Association of Maryland, Inc.

Health

- First Call for Help
- Health Care for the Homeless
- Jai Medical Center
- Maryland Youth Crisis Hotline
- Rape Crisis Center
- Sisters Together and Reaching, Inc.
- The Men's Health Center
- Black Educational AIDS Project

Housing

- 20th Street Hope House
- AIDS Interfaith Residential Services
- At Jacob's Well
- Baltimore Rescue Mission
- Cottage Avenue Community Transitional Housing
- Helping Up Mission
- Light Street Housing
- Maryland Re-Entry Program
- Safe Haven
- Salvation Army

Legal

- Homeless Persons Representation Project
- House of Ruth, Domestic Violence Legal Clinic
- Lawyer Referral & Information Service
- Legal Aid Bureau
- Office of the Public Defender
- University of Baltimore School of Law

Mental Health

- Baltimore Crisis Response Center
- Department of Social Services
- Family Help Line
- Gamblers Anonymous
- North Baltimore Center
- People Encouraging People
- Suicide Prevention Hotline
- You Are Never Alone

Substance Abuse

- Bright Hope House
- I Can't, We Can, Inc.
- Addict Referral and Counseling Center
- Crossroads Center
- Day Break Rehabilitation Program
- Friendship House
- SAFE House

Food and Clothing

- Salvation Army
- Bethel Outreach Center, Inc.
- Our Daily Bread
- Paul's Place

Baltimore has also initiated a transitional jobs project, Project Bridge, for ex-offenders. It's a collaborative effort involving Goodwill Industries of the Chesapeake; Associated Catholic Charities; the Center for Fathers, Families, and Workforce Development; and the Second Chance Project. Targeted toward ex-offenders who are unlikely to find employment on their own, the project provides eligible ex-offenders returning to Baltimore with transitional employment, support services, and job placement, followed by 12 months of post-placement retention services.

Community Resources

Many large communities, especially New York City, Chicago, Detroit, Houston, Los Angeles, and Washington, DC, offer various types of assistance programs for ex-offenders. If you have Internet access, you can quickly locate such programs and services in your community. For an excellent summary of governmental agencies and community-based organizations assisting ex-offenders with employment, legal, and other re-entry issues, including referrals to other relevant organizations, be sure to visit the **National H.I.R.E. Network** website, which provides access to resources in all 50 states:

<u>www.hirenetwork.org/resource.html</u>

Other useful websites include:

Government

- **Center for Employment Opportunities** (New York City) — <u>www.CEOworks.org</u>
- **Federal Bureau of Prisons** — <u>www.bop.gov</u>
- **U.S. Parole Commission** — <u>www.usdoj.gov/uspc/parole.htm</u>
- **U.S. Office of Justice Programs** — <u>www.ojp.usdoj.gov/reentry</u>
- **U.S. Department of Labor, Center for Faith-Based and Community Initiatives** — <u>www.dol-tlc.org</u>
- **Volunteers of America** — <u>www.voa.org</u>

Associations

- American Correctional Association   www.aca.org
- American Jail Association   www.corrections.com/aja.index.shtml
- Corrections Connection   www.corrections.com

Nonprofit/Volunteer

- The Safer Foundation   www.saferfoundation.org
- OPEN, INC.   www.openinc.org
- Just the Necessities   www.justthenecessities.org
- The Sentencing Project   www.sentencingproject.org
- Family and Corrections Network   www.fcnetwork.com
- Legal Action Center   www.lac.org
- Criminal Justice Policy Foundation   www.cjpf.org/clemency/clemency.html
- Annie E. Casey Foundation   www.aecf.org
- The Fortune Society   www.fortunesociety.org
- Second Chance/STRIVE (San Diego)   www.secondchanceprogram.org

Faith-Based

- Prison Fellowship Ministries   www.pfm.org
- Re-entry Prison and Jail Ministry   www.reentry.org/cgi-bin/resource.cfm #resources
- Conquest Offender Reintegration Ministries (Washington, DC)   www.conquesthouse.org/links.html
- Breakthrough Urban Ministries (Chicago)   www.breakthroughministries.com
- Exodus Transitional Community, Inc. (New York)   www.etcny.org

Identifying Your Community Resources

What is different among communities is the degree to which a community actually recognizes the need to focus on ex-offender re-entry issues. If you enter a community that does not provide specific assistance and services to ex-offenders, you'll be on your own in a sea of government agencies and community-based organizations that primarily provide employment and safety net services for disadvantaged groups, similar to the ones we identified on pages 29-30. Therefore, one of your most important initial jobs will be to understand how your particular community is structured in terms of such networks and relationships. You want to put specific names to the various categories of organizations we outlined in the figure on page 28. Once you understand your community, you should be prepared to take advantage of the many services and opportunities available to someone in your situation.

You can start identifying your community networks by completing the exercise on pages 32-33. Specify the actual names of up to five different government agencies and community-based organizations for each category that you need to know about and possibly use in the coming weeks and months. Remember the three types of organizations we identified on page 27 – government, nonprofit/volunteer, and church/faith-based. If you don't have this information on your community, ask your P.O. for assistance, visit your local library and ask personnel at the information desk for assistance, do an Internet search, or contact your local government social services department.

Identify Your Community Safety Nets and Opportunity Networks

My target community: _____

Employment Groups

1. _____
2. _____
3. _____
4. _____
5. _____

Housing Groups

1. _____
2. _____
3. _____
4. _____
5. _____

Food and Clothing Groups

1. _____
2. _____
3. _____
4. _____
5. _____

Health Care Groups

1. _____
2. _____
3. _____
4. _____
5. _____

Mental Health Groups (if an issue)

1. _____
2. _____
3. _____
4. _____
5. _____

Substance Abuse Groups (if an issue)

1. _____
2. _____
3. _____
4. _____
5. _____

Legal Groups

1. _____
2. _____
3. _____
4. _____
5. _____

Other Groups

1. _____
2. _____
3. _____
4. _____
5. _____

The Importance of One-Stop Career Centers

One community group you should become familiar with is your local One-Stop Career Center. Indeed, make sure you visit a One-Stop Career Center soon after release. It may well become one of your most important lifelines for landing your first job out.

Usually operated by the state employment office, One-Stop Career Centers provide numerous resources for assisting individuals in finding employment, such as computerized job banks, job listings, counseling and assessment services, job search assistance, and training programs. Since career professionals staffing these centers increasingly work with ex-offenders, you'll be no stranger to their offices. Be sure to disclose your background to their personnel, since knowing about your criminal record may result in their providing you with special contacts and services. The personnel in many of the centers regularly work with ex-offenders and thus know ex-offender-friendly employers. In fact, you may find one staff member whose job is to work with ex-offenders. You can easily find the center nearest you by visiting this website:

- One-Stop Career Centers   www.careeronestop.org

If you're using the Internet, you'll also want to visit these two related websites operated by the U.S. Department of Labor:

- America's CareerInfoNet   www.acinet.org
- America's Service Locator   www.servicelocator.org

Consider Using Temporary Employment Agencies

You also may want to contact various temporary employment agencies or staffing firms. This is good way to quickly get employed and acquire work experience. With temporary employment agencies, you work for the agency which, in turn, places you on temporary assignments with their clients. While these companies primarily recruit individuals for temporary or part-time positions, many of these firms also have temp-to-perm programs. With these programs, you may work two to three months with one employer who may decide to hire you full-time once your contract expires with the temporary employment agency if you have met their performance expectations. Many large cities have over 200 such firms operating. Many of these agencies specialize in particular occupations, such as construction, accounting, information technology, law, and health services. Other agencies may recruit for all types of positions, including many low-skill, low-wage labor positions. Some of the most popular temporary employment agencies with a nationwide presence include:

- Labor Finders   www.laborfinders.com
- Manpower   www.manpower.com
- Olsten   www.olsten.com
- Kelly Services   www.kellyservices.com

Map Your Safety Nets and Opportunity Networks

Create a picture of the safety nets and opportunities networks in your community by completing the figure on page 35. This is a blank version of our example on page 28. Put the names of the most important groups you identified on pages 32-33 as well as additional ones we've discussed on pages 33-34. Also, include the names of any individuals who could be key to finding a job. We'll later identify such individuals when we examine your network in Chapter 11.

Community Safety Nets and Opportunity Networks

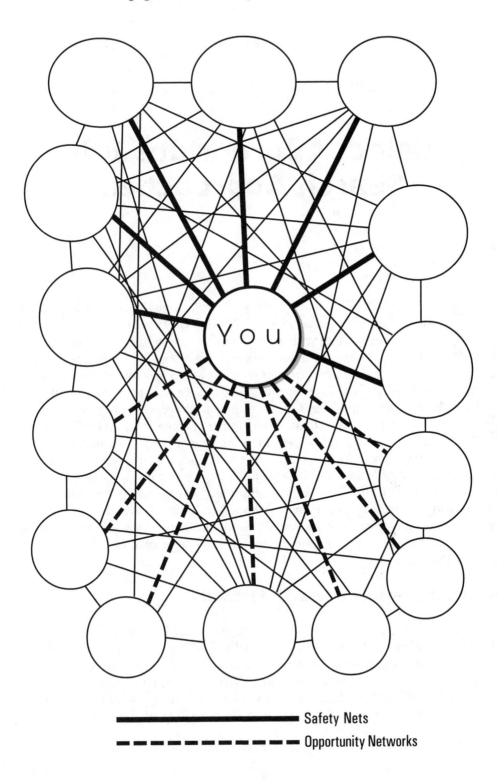

Safety Nets
Opportunity Networks

6

Select Appropriate Job Search Approaches

H OW DO YOU PLAN TO find a job? Are you planning to look for a job on your own or rely on others for help? Will you primarily respond to classified ads in the newspaper with a letter and resume or visit companies to fill out applications? Do you plan to knock on doors to introduce yourself to employers or hang around a busy corner for someone to hire you for the day? What about using the telephone to call employers, or searching for jobs on the Internet? Will you look for jobs through a One-Stop Career Center, employment agencies, placement services, or friends and family? Do you plan to attend a job fair or some other type of career event?

Most anyone can find a job, especially in an economy where demand for workers outstrips available supply. You can always rake leaves, trim lawns, clean buildings, paint, lift boxes, drive a vehicle, pick up trash, or use a shovel. The real questions are (1) what type of work you will find? and (2) how rewarding will the job be in terms of salary, benefits, and job satisfaction? How you approach your job search will make a big difference in what type of work you will do as well as the next job you may move to in your worklife. If you choose an appropriate job search approach, you should be able to find a job that's right for you.

Choose the Best Job Search Methods

There is no one best way to find a job. In fact, every day hundreds of people find jobs using a variety of methods. However, some methods are more effective than others.

The best methods are ones that lead to good paying jobs with a future – not just any job. Studies consistently show that the most effective job search method (used by 50 to 80 percent of successful candidates) is **networking** – finding job leads through family, friends, and acquaintances. The job search experiences of ex-offenders also confirm this finding – those who quickly enter the job market do so through the assistance of family and friends. We'll discuss this important, and often misunderstood, method at the end of the chapter as well as in Chapter 11.

The least effective job search method, which is the most widely used method, is responding to classified ads and job postings.

If you want to use your time wisely, focus the greatest amount of your time on those methods that appear to have the greatest payoff in terms of job leads and interviews.

Respond to Classified Ads

Pick up any newspaper and thumb through the classified ad section in search of a job related to your interests, skills, and experience. Chances are you will identify several interesting jobs, but few of them will relate to your skills and experience. Believing that most job vacancies are found in the newspapers, thousands of job seekers explore the classified ads each day. Engaging in wishful thinking, they often respond to ads with a resume, letter, or phone call. When they don't get a positive reply, many conclude there are no jobs for them. Many become disillusioned and have difficulty keeping positive and motivated to continue their job search.

Your chances of getting a job by responding to classified ads are not very good – at best a five percent chance of getting a positive or negative response from each employer you contact! Here's the truth about classified job ads:

1. **They represent no more than 15 percent of available job vacancies.** Some of the remaining 85 percent of job vacancies may be advertised elsewhere (on the Internet, in employment offices, on bulletin boards, with unions), but most of the jobs (50 to 75 percent) are found on the "hidden job market," which primarily operates by word-of-mouth and are found through networking.

2. **They tend to represent jobs at the two extreme ends of the job market** – low-wage, high-turnover positions and high-wage, highly skilled positions. In other words, they represent difficult-to-fill positions. Most jobs, which fall between these two extremes, are not well represented in the classifieds.

3. **They create unrealistic expectations – false hopes** that you will actually get the job or that you are basically unqualified for most jobs.

Our point here is that you should not waste a great deal of time focused on classified ads. It's an ego-bruising experience to get rejected by many employers. Explore classified ads for a few minutes each day, respond to a few that look promising, but move on to more productive job search methods that involve fewer rejections.

If you see a job in that classifieds that seems to be a perfect fit, you can increase your odds of getting a job interview by doing the following:

1. **Respond immediately** with a phone call in which you ask for an interview.

2. **Follow the application instructions.** How does the employer want you to contact him – by e-mail, fax, or mail your resume or call for a telephone

screening interview? What does he want you to send him – resume, letter, references, examples of work?

3. **Dissect the ad carefully and then write a cover letter** in which you respond to each requirement with corresponding examples of your qualifications. If you applying for a position as an electrician, your letter might include the following statements:

Your Requirements	My Qualifications
■ One year experience	Completed one-year apprenticeship and served two years as an electrician's helper on complex commercial projects
■ Responsible	Praised by previous employer and co-workers as being a quick starter who takes initiative, is responsible, and gets the job done well and on time.

4. **Follow up your application within five days** with a phone call. This will be the single most important action you can take to move your application to the top of the pile and get it read and remembered. Ask if the employer has any questions about your application, restate your qualifications and interest in the position, and ask for a job interview. If you don't ask for the job interview, chances are the employer won't contact you for an interview! Your phone call also gives you a chance to be interviewed over the telephone by the employer – the first screening step in the job interview process.

If you take these actions, your chances of getting a job interview should increase considerably. Indeed, you may just get lucky and land a job through the classifieds!

Use the Internet

During the past 10 years the Internet has become a very popular resource for both employers and job seekers. In fact, much of today's job market and recruitment/job search activities have moved to the Internet. If you are not using the Internet in your job search, you are not up-to-date in your job search, and you will be missing out on important segments of the job market. In addition, employers may view you as unprepared for today's workplace, which increasingly values technical skills.

Many employers use the Internet to recruit candidates through employment websites, such as Monster.com and Careerbuilder.com, as well as through their own company websites. Job seekers use the Internet to find job vacancies, post their resumes to online resume databases, and research jobs, companies, and employers. Today, approximately 15 percent of job seekers actually find jobs based upon using the Internet – a percentage that continues to increase each year.

In many respects, using the Internet is similar to finding a job through classified ads. In fact, many classified ads appear on employment websites and are called "job postings." Employers who might normally place classified ads for positions in newspapers find it's cheaper and more effective to post their jobs on websites. They also find resume databases useful for identifying candidates who best meet their hiring requirements.

The largest and most popular employment websites provide a wealth of information for job seekers about jobs, employers, and the job search in general: job search tips, featured articles, career experts, career assessment tests, community forums, chat groups, salary calculators, resume and interview advice, relocation information, success stories, newsletters, career events, online job fairs, polls and surveys, contests, online education and training, company ads, and special channels for students, freelancers, military, and other groups. If you have Internet access, you should explore these major employment websites:

- www.ajb.org
- www.monster.com
- www.careerbuilder.com
- www.careerjournal.com
- www.directemployers.com
- http://hotjobs.yahoo.com
- www.nationjob.com
- www.careerflex.com
- www.employment911.com

Altogether, over 25,000 websites focus on employment. Hundreds of thousands of additional employer websites include information on employment with specific companies and organizations.

However, you should be aware that jobs found on the Internet tend to be for individuals with at least a high school education and some college. Individuals lacking a high school education, work experience, and marketable skills are unlikely to find employers on the Internet interested in their backgrounds for two reasons: (1) they don't have such jobs, and (2) it's cheaper to recruit low-wage earners by putting a sign on a busy street corner, in a window, or at a work site; visiting day-laborer centers; or listing the job free of charge with a public employment office or through a job developer working with hard-to-place individuals. If you lack basic education, work experience, and skills, you should use the Internet to primarily educate yourself about alternative jobs and careers, assess your skills, and learn how to acquire more education and training.

If you don't have a computer or an Internet connection, contact your local library or One-Stop Career Center for assistance. Most of these places offer free Internet access and some minimal help to get you up and running on the Internet.

Even though you may not qualify for jobs found on the Internet, learn how to use the Internet early in your job search. It will open a whole new world of employment to you as well as give you many great ideas for thinking about and planning your future.

While the Internet can be extremely useful for job seekers, few of them know how to use this tool properly. Many mistakenly believe that employers actually hire over the Internet! When you are looking for a job, the Internet is best used for:

- Conducting research on jobs, employers, companies, and communities.

- Acquiring useful advice and referrals.

- Communicating with individuals via e-mail.

Your most productive online activities will relate to **research** and **communication**. While you may, depending on your qualifications, want to post your resume on various employment websites and periodically review online job listings, don't spend a great deal of time doing so and then waiting to hear from employers based on such activities. This whole process is similar to answering classified employment ads in newspapers – a low probability of getting a response from employers. Move on to other more productive activities, especially visiting **employer websites**, which are more likely to yield useful information, job listings, and applications than the more general and popular employment websites.

But your most useful online job search activity relates to **research**. Thousands of websites can yield useful information for enhancing your job search. For example, use the Internet to explore different jobs (www.bls.gov/oco) and employers (www.hoovers.com), community-based employment assistance (www.careeronestop.org), career counselors (www.nbcc.org), networking groups (www.linkedin.com), salary ranges (www.salary.com), best communities (www.findyourspot.com), relocation (www.monstermoving.com), job search tips (www.winningthejob.com), and career advice (www.wetfeet.com). You can even use the Internet to conduct an online assessment (www.careerlab.com), blast your resume to thousands of employers (www.resumeblaster.com), contact recruiters (www.recruiters online.com), and explore hundreds of professional associations (www.ipl.org/div/aon) and nonprofit organizations (www.guidestar.org) that are linked to thousands of employers.

The Internet also is a terrific way to **communicate** with people, especially with employers. If you don't have an e-mail address, you can always set up a free e-mail account through one of the major search engines:

- **Google**   http://mail.google.com
- **MSN**   www.hotmail.com
- **Yahoo**   www.yahoo.com

For more information on how to wisely use the Internet in your job search, see Ron and Caryl Krannich's *America's Top Internet Job Sites* (Impact Publications), Margaret Dikel's *Job Searching on the Internet* (McGraw-Hill), and Richard Nelson Bolles's *Job Hunting on the Internet* (Ten Speed Press).

Contact Employers Directly

One of the most effective methods for finding a job is making direct contact with employers. You can do this many different ways:

- **Use the telephone:** Few people enjoy making cold calls to strangers, especially since doing so results in many rejections. However, job seekers who contact numerous employers by phone do generate job interviews. In fact, this is the fastest way to get job interviews. Make 100 phone calls to inquire about job vacancies and you may be able to generate one or two job interviews. Since this is largely a numbers game, and you are playing the odds, you must be willing to make many phone calls and endure numerous rejections. Most people you call will politely tell you they have no jobs available at present. But persistence will pay off. You will eventually uncover job vacancies for which you qualify. Use the Yellow Pages as your directory for identifying potential employers. When making such calls, have a prepared outline of points to cover in front of you from which you (1) quickly introduce yourself, (2) ask about job vacancies, (3) request a job interview, and (4) thank the person for his or her time and consideration. Don't write it out word for word and read it. If you do this, you will sound as if you are reading it. You want to sound spontaneous. If you receive a rejection, that's okay. In the process, you may acquire some useful information about jobs elsewhere. And you can now move on to call the next potential employer!

- **Send e-mail:** If you use the Internet, you should explore the websites of employers. While many of these websites will post employment opportunities, others may not. If they don't, send an e-mail inquiring about such opportunities. However, if you can find a phone number, it's best to make a telephone call rather than wait for an e-mail reply. Many companies automatically delete unsolicited e-mail inquiries. E-mail is no substitute for using the telephone, which is more efficient and effective than e-mail.

- **Go door to door:** Many job seekers are successful in finding jobs by literally showing up at the doors or work sites of employers and asking about job opportunities. This approach requires a great deal of initiative, entrepreneurship, and a willingness to accept rejections as part of the game. This is the in-your-face version of the cold telephone call. Many businesses, such as large retail stores (Wal-Mart, K-Mart, Target, Home Depot), grocery stores, restaurants, and banks, are well organized to handle walk-in applicants. You may be asked to sit at a computer terminal or "job kiosk" to complete an electronic application, or you will be given a paper application to complete. Others, such as construction firms, often welcome individuals to show up at their job sites for work. If you walk into a small business, such as a warehouse, auto repair shop, or construction company, you may be able to meet directly with the owner and ask about job opportunities. Timing is the key to such walk-in approaches – if you happen to arrive at the right time, when a job needs to be filled immediately, you may get lucky and be offered the job. If that happens, be prepared to interview (see Chapter 12) for a job while inquiring about opportunities. If you use this approach, be prepared for many rejections. However, if you persist and visit 100 employers, chances are you will uncover one or two job opportunities for which you qualify. If you visit 500 employers, you may uncover five job opportunities.

- **Hang around busy corners:** Day-laborer sites, both formal and informal, are used a great deal by illegal immigrants and individuals with limited skills and education. Day-laborer sites may be found on a busy street corner or adjacent to a convenience store or vacant lot. Large day-laborer markets of Hispanics (*jornaleros*) are especially prevalent in Southern California, Arizona, Texas, and Florida where they have recently become very controversial political issues. Employers – usually home owners or subcontractors who need cheap day laborers – may stop to check who is available for a few hours or a day or two of temporary work. Most work is physical labor – landscaping, roofing, gardening, construction – and wages are usually negotiated on an hourly, daily, or per job basis. In many communities, informal day-laborer sites represent a gray market of undocumented workers (illegal immigrants) and cash wages (no tax or Social Security deductions). Cities in some states, such as California, Washington, Arizona, Illinois, New York, Connecticut, Maryland, Georgia, Florida, and Washington, DC, actually sponsor formal day-laborer sites where employers can come to hire laborers.

Despite controversies concerning the illegal immigrant and taxation questions, day-laborer centers offer employment options for poor people who lack sufficient education and skills, and who are willing to tolerate unstable and often exploitative work (many are cheated by unscrupulous employers) situations. In fact, some studies show that nearly 25 percent of day laborers prefer such unstable work situations to other types of employment. Many can make $80 to $100 or more a day by just showing up when they want to work. In some cases day laborer experiences turn into full-time jobs, especially with subcontractors who decide to hire the best of the many day laborers they have worked with and thus have a chance to screen their on-the-job behavior.

Register With Employment Agencies and Placement Services

Public employment services operate One-Stop Career Centers (www.careeronestop.org), which post many vacancies listed by employers in their communities. These centers also are linked to America's Job Bank (www.ajb.dni.us), an electronic job bank which includes over 1 million job listings.

Many employment agencies and placement services look for candidates they can place with their clients. Registering with these agencies and services can result in temporary or permanent jobs. However, beware of any agency or service that wants you to pay them for employment services. The legitimate firms are paid by employers – not by job seekers.

Two of the best known temporary labor and staffing firms found in hundreds of communities across the country are LaborFinders (www.laborfinders.com) and Manpower (www.manpower.com). You may want to visit these firms early in your job search since they may be able to help you quickly find employment with their many clients. Also, check on dozens of other temporary employment firms that may operate in your community.

If your community has a specialized program to assist ex-offenders, chances are they also have a placement program designed to quickly place ex-offenders in jobs with employers who are interested in hiring ex-offenders.

If you are a college graduate, you can use the placement services of the career center or alumni office. For recent college graduates this means signing up for on-campus job interviews through the career services center.

Attend Job Fairs

Job fairs are great ways to survey job opportunities, meet employers, network, practice resume and interview skills, learn about salaries and benefits, and possibly get hired on the spot. While you will find many job fairs operating in large cities (check the classified section of your Sunday newspaper for large ads announcing such events), many correctional institutions also sponsor job fairs for ex-offenders.

The typical job fair is held in a large conference room of a hotel or a public building and takes place over one day – often from 9am to 4pm. Many employers have representatives at tables or booths who advertise their company or organization and are looking for candidates who meet their hiring requirements. Job seekers circulate among the various displays (booths and tables) as they try to learn more about the organizations, pick up literature, talk with a representative, and leave a resume. Job fairs can be very enlightening experiences for job seekers, especially if they find a good selection of employers and if the job fair also includes special job search workshops, such as writing resumes, interviewing for jobs, or using a job fair in your job search.

Job fairs for ex-offenders are great places to find employment since employers already indicate, by their participation, that they are willing to hire ex-offenders. However, employers attending such job fairs are not looking for just any ex-offenders – they want to hire the best of the best who have basic education and workplace skills.

You should keep the following eight tips in mind when planning to attend a job fair:

- **Check to see if you qualify for the job fair.** Some job fairs are open to the general public and involve many different types of employers. These general job fairs are sometimes sponsored by a single company that is opening a new business and needs to recruit hundreds of people, such as a large hotel and conference center, sports arena, or an amusement park, Many job fairs specialize in a particular skill or occupational area. For example, some job fairs only focus on high-tech and computer skills. Others may specialize in clerical skills or the construction trades. And still others may be organized for government-related jobs, including specialized job fairs of government contractors looking for individuals with military backgrounds as well as those with security clearances. Special career events, such as career conferences sponsored by a single company, may be by invitation only.

- **Be sure to pre-register for the job fair.** Many job fairs require you to register before the event – not just show up at the door. One of the registration requirements is to submit a resume which, in turn, is entered into a resume database. This database enables employers attending the job fair to review the resumes online both before and after the job fair.

- **Plan ahead.** Prior to attending the event, try to get a list of companies that will be attending. Research several of the companies on the Internet. Discover what they do, whom they employ, and what is particularly unique or different about them. When you go the job fair, you will have some knowledge of those employers you want to meet. Better still, you'll impress the representatives when you indicate you know something about what they do. You'll avoid asking that killer question – *"What do you do?"* Being prepared in this manner also means you will be more at ease in talking with employers, because you have some common ground knowledge for engaging in an intelligent job-oriented conversation.

- **Bring copies of your resume to the job fair.** Since you will be meeting many employers at the job fair as you circulate from one table or booth to another, your calling card is your resume. A good rule of thumb is to bring 25 to 50 copies of your resume to the job fair. If the employer is interested in you, they will want to see your resume. Best of all, they will give you instant feedback on your qualifications. In many cases, they will interview you on the spot and may even hire you that day! So make sure you write a terrific resume as well as bring enough copies for every employer you are interesting in meeting.

- **Dress appropriately.** Job fairs are places where first impressions are very important. Be sure to dress as if you were going to a formal job interview – conservative, neat, and clean. If, for example, you have tattoos on your arm, be sure to wear a long-sleeve shirt. While your tattoo may be a great conversation piece with some friends and strangers, they are a negative distraction for many employers, who may question your branding choices.

- **Prepare a 30-second pitch.** Your 30-second pitch should tell an employer who you are and what skills and experience you have that should be of interest to the employer. Tell them why they should consider interviewing and hiring you.

- **Be prepared to interview for the job.** Since some employers will actually interview candidates and hire them at the job fair, don't assume a job fair is merely a casual "get together" to just meet employers. Prepare for a job fair in the same way you would prepare for a job interview – bring a positive attitude, be enthusiastic and energetic, anticipate questions, prepare your own questions, and observe all the verbal and nonverbal rules for interview success (see Chapter 12).

- **Follow up your contacts within five days.** Job fairs are all about networking with employers. If you're interested in an employer and you've had a chance to meet a representative and get his or her name and business card, be sure to follow up with a phone call and/or e-mail within five days of your meeting. This communication will remind the individual of your continuing interest and may result in a formal job interview with other company representatives.

Network With Family, Friends, and Others

As we noted earlier, the single most effective way of getting a job is through networking. Your network consists of family, friends, your P.O., former supervisor, acquaintances, minister, people you do business with, and even strangers whom you meet and with whom you develop a relationship. These people can be of assistance in finding a job, because many have useful information, advice, and referrals to others who know about jobs appropriate for you. You want to plug into these informal yet rich channels of job information and communications.

Since most jobs are not advertised, through networking you should be able to tap into the **hidden job market** where many of the best jobs can be found. These jobs are located through word-of-mouth. People in your network – family friends, P.O., and others – know about such jobs, or they may know people who may know, and thus they refer you to others in the know. The more networking you do, the more likely you will find a job on the hidden job market.

However, many people are reluctant to network because it involves initiating conversations and meetings with others. The twin fears of embarrassment (I'm unemployed and an ex-offender) and rejection (they may say *"No, I can't help you"*) work against many ex-offenders. But these are false fears that seldom materialize. Instead, people who learn to network properly are surprised how supportive others are in giving them useful information, advice, and referrals. Many of these people have been in similar situations and others helped them with their job search. Most people enjoy helping others, as long as they are not put on the spot and asked to take responsibility for your employment fate! Networkers are not beggars – they are nice people who are in search of information, advice, and hopefully useful referrals to people who have the power to hire.

We devote Chapter 11 to the whole process of networking in the job search. We show you how to launch an effective networking campaign. Read it carefully and put it into practice immediately. It may well become your most important approach to landing a job that's right for you!

Use Your Time Wisely

Based on our previous discussion of the best methods for finding a job, how do you plan to organize your job search and use your time? Identify the job search methods you plan to use during your first 30 days. List the methods it the order of importance as well as assign what percentage of your job search time you plan to devote to each methods:

My Best Job Search Methods

Rank	Method	Percent of Time (100%)
1	_____	_____
2	_____	_____
3	_____	_____
4	_____	_____
5	_____	_____
6	_____	_____
7	_____	_____
8	_____	_____

Once you've completed this exercise, have a counselor or trusted acquaintance examine your plan. Ask them the following questions:

1. Have I identified the most important job search methods appropriate for the types of jobs I'm seeking?

2. Am I using my time wisely for each of these methods?

3. Are there better ways to use my job search time?

In so doing, you should receive useful feedback for better planning your job search. Whatever you do, use your time wisely by focusing the most time on those activities that are likely to produce the best results.

7

Assess Your Skills and Identify Your MAS

ISCOVERING WHO YOU ARE AND what you really want to do are essential for conducting an effective job search. It requires assessing your interests, skills, and abilities, which are the basis for identifying your pattern of motivated abilities and skills (MAS), and relating this information to a job objective (Chapter 8).

You must be brutally **honest** with yourself. No games, no tricks, no lies, no manipulation, no scamming – just the truth about you. This truth may initially hurt, but it, too, will set you free as you go on to landing a good job and leading a productive life based on an understanding of your unique talents. It will have a surprising effect on your self-esteem – you will actually meet a new you who has lots of good things to say about you. Best of all, your self-assessment may transform you from the person you thought you were to the person you want to be.

Ask Powerful Questions About Yourself

Through a series of probing questions and exercises, your self-assessment activities enable you to answer this two-part question:

*What do I **do well** and **enjoy doing**?*

This question focuses on **specifying your interests, skills, and abilities** and prepares you for answering the next critical question:

*What do I **really** want to do?*

When you answer this question, you are prepared to **state your job or career objective**. Taken together, these two questions will help you organize a powerful job search that clearly focuses on your major strengths and goals.

What Employers Want From You

It's not surprising what employers want from their employees – truthfulness, character, and value. They want to better **predict your future behavior** based upon a clear understanding of your past patterns of behavior. You can help them achieve this understanding by organizing this step in your job search around the qualities of truthfulness, character, and value.

Employers want to hire individuals who are competent, intelligent, honest, enthusiastic, and likable. At the same time, many employers are suspicious of candidates, because they have encountered manipulators, scammers, and deceivers among job applicants.

While employers may appear to trust what you say, they also want to verify your credentials and observe what you actually do. This means conducting background checks (over 95 percent of employers do this), asking probing behavior-based questions, subjecting candidates to multiple job interviews, and administering a variety of revealing tests (aptitude, drug, personality, psychological, and polygraph) to discover the truth about you. **Verification and observation** are the real basis for trust – not questionable resumes and clever conversations with strangers.

Above all, employers want **value** for their money – people who can do the job well. The most highly valued candidates demonstrate strong communication skills, honesty/integrity, interpersonal/teamwork skills, and a strong work ethic. As an ex-offender, you need to make sure these highly desired skills are part of your skill set and clearly communicate them to employers.

At this stage in your job search, it's extremely important that you take a complete inventory of your skills so you can better communicate with employers what it is you do well and enjoy doing. Once you do this and formulate a clear objective, which you will do in the next chapter, you will be on the road to finding the right job for you.

Your Skills and Abilities

Most people possess two types of skills that define their strengths as well as enable them to move within the job market: work-content skills and functional skills. These skills become the key **language** – both verbs and nouns – for communicating your qualifications to employers through your resumes and letters as well as in interviews.

We assume you have already acquired certain **work-content skills**. These "hard skills" are easy to recognize since they are often identified as "qualifications" for **specific** jobs. Work-content skills tend to be technical and job-specific in nature. Examples of such skills include welding, painting, cooking, cleaning, landscaping, repairing air conditioners, programming computers, selling real estate, wiring a room, or operating a complicated piece of machinery. They may require formal training, are associated with specific trades or professions, and are used only in certain job settings. While these skills do not transfer well from one occupation to another, they are critical for entering and advancing within specific occupations.

At the same time, you possess many **functional/transferable skills** employers readily seek along with work-content skills. These are "soft skills" associated with **numerous** job settings. They are mainly acquired through experience rather than formal training, and can be communicated through a general vocabulary. Functional/transferable skills are less easy to recognize since they tend to be linked to certain **personal characteristics** (energetic, intelligent, likable) and the ability to **deal with processes** (communicating, problem-solving, motivating) rather than **doing things** (programming a computer, building a house, repairing air conditioners).

Ex-offenders as a group possess few marketable occupational skills, because of their youth, limited education, and spotty work experience. If, on the other hand, you have participated in pre-release education and vocational programs, you will have some work-content skills to include on your applications, in your resume, and during job interviews.

The skills we identify and help you organize in this chapter are the functional skills that define your **strengths**. While most people have only a few work-content skills, they may have numerous – as many as 300 – functional/transferable skills. These skills enable job seekers to more easily change jobs and careers without acquiring additional education and training. They constitute an important bridge for moving from one occupation to another. But you must first be aware of your functional skills before you can relate them to the job market.

Focus on Key Strengths and Questions

If you begin your job search by focusing on your **strengths**, you'll be able to quickly identify your work-content and functional skills. If you focus on overcoming your weaknesses, chances are you will waste a great deal of energy on things you can not easily change. While you should be aware of your weaknesses, your strengths give you needed direction and keep you focused on what's really important to employers.

Two of the most humbling questions you may encounter in your job search are *"Why should I hire you?"* and *"What are your weaknesses?"* While employers may not directly ask these questions, they ask them nonetheless. If you can't answer these questions in a positive manner – directly, indirectly, verbally, or nonverbally – your job search will likely founder, and you will join the ranks of the unsuccessful and disillusioned job searchers who feel something is wrong with them. Ex-offenders and individuals who have lost their jobs are particularly vulnerable to these questions, since many have lowered self-esteem and self-image as a result of their situations. Many such people focus on what is wrong rather than what is right about themselves, which tends to be self-destructive. By all means avoid such negative thinking!

Employers want to hire your **value or strengths** – not your weaknesses. Since it is easier to identify and interpret weaknesses, employers look for indicators of your strengths by trying to identify your weaknesses. The more successful you are in communicating your strengths to employers, the better off you will be in relation to both employers and fellow applicants.

Your Strengths and Weaknesses

Unfortunately, many people work against their own best interests. Not knowing their strengths, they market their weaknesses by first identifying job vacancies and then trying to fit their "qualifications" into job descriptions. This approach often frustrates applicants; it presents a picture of a job market which is not interested in the applicant's strengths and it generates the often-heard complaint of frustrated job seekers – *"No one will hire me!"* This experience leads some people to acquire new skills which they hope will be marketable, even though they do not enjoy using them. Millions of individuals find themselves in such misplaced situations: the office worker who would rather be working outdoors with animals; the divorce lawyer who would rather be teaching in a university; the computer programmer who enjoys cooking and would love to be a top chef; the surgeon who is an accomplished pianist; or the salesman who is good at managing a community fund-raising drive. Your task is to avoid joining the ranks of the misplaced and unhappy workforce by first understanding your skills and then relating them to your values, interests, and goals. In so doing, you will be in a better position to target your job search toward jobs that should become especially rewarding and fulfilling.

Your Functional/Transferable Skills

If you are an ex-offender with limited work experience and few strengths, you especially need to understand and identify your transferable or functional skills. Once you have done this, you will be better prepared to identify what it is you want to do. Moreover, your self-image and self-esteem will improve. Better still, you will be prepared to communicate your strengths to others through a rich skills-based vocabulary. These outcomes are critically important for completing applications and writing your resume and letters (Chapter 10) as well as for networking and interviewing (Chapters 11 and 12).

Let's illustrate the concept of functional/transferable skills for ex-offenders who are currently incarcerated. Many of them view their skills in strict work-content terms – knowledge of a particular job or a specific education and training experience, such as cleaning buildings, dishwashing, cooking, repairing radios, working in the laundry, grounds keeping, landscaping, repairing machinery, welding, fixing air conditioners, plumbing, using computers, or making furniture. While there are many general labor and trade jobs on the outside directly related to these prison experiences (carpentry, construction, janitorial work, kitchen jobs, culinary work, electrical work, automotive repair, office work, pipefitting, welding, and electronic), many other jobs may relate to your transferable skills which may be your major strengths.

Ex-offenders possess several skills that are directly transferable to a variety of jobs. Unaware of these skills, they may fail to communicate their strengths to others. For example, if you have participated in educational and vocational programs, you may have demonstrated several of the following **transferable organizational and interpersonal skills:**

1. Communication
2. Decision-making
3. Following orders/instructions
4. Selling/persuading
5. Logical thinking
6. Team building/playing
7. Organizing/prioritizing
8. Reviewing/evaluating
9. Trouble-shooting
10. Problem solving

In addition, you may have demonstrated some of these **transferable personality and work-style traits** sought by employers in many occupational fields:

1. Quick learner/astute
2. Diligent/patient
3. Honest/trustworthy
4. Loyal/motivated
5. Patient/calm

6. Punctual/reliable
7. Assertive/initiative
8. Responsible/cooperative
9. Intelligent/sensitive
10. Accurate/talented

If you have done a good job, your supervisor will likely focus on complimenting you about these skills and traits, which also gives your P.O. some idea of your major strengths. Both individuals may be important to your job search, especially when it comes time to provide references.

As just noted, most functional/transferable skills can be classified into these two general skills and trait categories – organizational/ interpersonal skills and personality/ work-style traits:

Organizational and Interpersonal Skills

___ communicating
___ trouble-shooting
___ problem solving
___ implementing
___ analyzing/assessing
___ self-understanding
___ planning
___ understanding
___ decision-making
___ setting goals
___ innovating
___ conceptualizing
___ thinking logically
___ generalizing
___ evaluating
___ managing time
___ identifying
      problems

___ creating
___ synthesizing
___ judging
___ forecasting
___ controlling
___ tolerating
      ambiguity
___ organizing
___ motivating
___ persuading
___ leading
___ encouraging
___ selling
___ improving
___ performing
___ designing
___ reviewing
___ consulting

___ attaining
___ teaching
___ team building
___ cultivating
___ updating
___ advising
___ coaching
___ training
___ supervising
___ interpreting
___ estimating
___ achieving
___ negotiating
___ reporting
___ administering
___ managing
___ multi-tasking
___ defending

Personality and Work-Style Traits

___ diligent
___ honest
___ patient
___ reliable
___ innovative
___ perceptive
___ persistent
___ assertive
___ tactful
___ sensitive
___ loyal
___ astute

___ successful
___ risk taker
___ versatile
___ easygoing
___ enthusiastic
___ calm
___ outgoing
___ flexible
___ expressive
___ competent
___ adaptable
___ punctual

___ democratic
___ receptive
___ resourceful
___ diplomatic
___ determinant
___ self-confident
___ creative
___ tenacious
___ open
___ discreet
___ objective
___ talented

__ warm	__ adventuresome	__ precise
__ empathic	__ cooperative	__ competent
__ orderly	__ firm	__ sophisticated
__ tidy	__ dynamic	__ diplomatic
__ tolerant	__ sincere	__ effective
__ candid	__ self-starter	__ efficient
__ frank	__ initiator	__ cool and collected

These are the types of skills and traits you need to identify and then communicate to employers in your resumes and letters as well as during interviews. Be sure to refer to these lists when you write your resume and letters and prepare for your job interview.

Identify Your Skills

You should take some vocational tests and psychological inventories to identify your values, interests, skills, aptitudes, and temperament. Most are pencil-and-paper or computerized tests which are administered and interpreted by a career professional. Several prisons, jails, and detention centers administer assessment devices as part of their pre-release programs. Once you enter your community, several of these inventories are available at low cost ($20) through the career services centers of local community colleges. Also, check with your local One-Stop Career Center for information on such inventories and tests.

The most widely used assessment devices are the *Myers-Briggs Type Indicator®*, *Strong Interest Inventory®*, *Self-Directed Search®*, and *Campbell™ Interest and Skill Survey (CISS®)*. If you have Internet access, you can find several other assessment devices online. The following seven websites are well worth exploring for both free and fee-based online assessment tools:

- **SkillsOne**   www.skillsone.com
  (CPP's online assessment system)   www.cpp-db.com
- **CareerLab.com**   www.careerlab.com
- **Self-Directed Search®**   www.self-directed-search.com
- **Personality Online**   www.personalityonline.com
- **Keirsey Character Sorter**   www.keirsey.com
- **MAPP™**   www.assessment.com
- **PersonalityType**   www.personalitytype.com

These 15 additional sites also include a wealth of related assessment devices that you can access online:

- **Analyze My Career**   www.analyzemycareer.com
- **Birkman Method**   www.birkman.com
- **Career Key**   www.careerkey.org/english
- **CareerLeader™**   www.careerleader.com
- **CareerPlanner.com**   www.careerplanner.com
- **CareerPerfect.com**   www.careerperfect.com
- **Careers By Design®**   www.careers-by-design.com
- **Enneagram**   www.ennea.com

- Humanmetrics   www.humanmetricsa.com
- Jackson Vocational
  Interest Inventory   www.jvis.com
- My Future   www.myfuture.com
- People Management
  International   www.sima-pmi.com
- Profiler   www.profiler.com
- QueenDom.com   www.queendom.com
- Tests on the Web   www.2h.com

We present several good alternatives to the above assessment devices in the remainder of this chapter that are designed to identify both your work-content and transferable skills and then relate them to your interests, values, and motivations. These self-assessment techniques stress your positives or strengths rather than identify your negatives or weaknesses. Each exercise requires a different investment of your time and effort as well as varying degrees of assistance from other people.

These exercises, however, should be used with caution. They provide you with a clear picture of your **past**, which may or may not be particularly useful for charting your future. Nonetheless, these exercises do help individuals:

- Organize data on themselves
- Target their job search around clear objectives and skills
- Generate a rich vocabulary of skills and accomplishments for communicating their strengths to potential employers.

If you feel these exercises are inadequate for your needs, by all means seek professional assistance from a testing or assessment center staffed by a licensed psychologist or certified career counselor. Many such centers can do in-depth testing which goes further than these self-directed skill exercises.

Checklist Method

This is the simplest method for identifying your strengths. Review the different types of transferable skills outlined on pages 50-51. Place a "1" in front of the skills that **strongly** characterize you; assign a "2" to those skills that describe you to a **large extent**; put a "3" before those that may or may not describe you to **some extent**. When finished, review the lists and identify, in order of importance, the top 10 characteristics that best describe you on each list.

Autobiography of Accomplishments

Write a lengthy essay about your **life accomplishments**. This could range from 10 to 15 pages. After completing the essay, go through it page by page to identify what you most enjoyed doing (working with different kinds of information, people, and things) and what skills you used most frequently as well as enjoyed using. Finally, identify those skills you wish to continue using. After analyzing and synthesizing this data, you should have a relatively clear picture of your strongest skills.

Computerized Assessment Programs

While the previous self-directed exercises required you to either respond to checklists of skills or reconstruct and analyze your past job experiences, several computerized self-assessment programs are designed to help individuals identify their skills. Many of the programs are available in career centers, and some can be accessed online. Some of the most widely used programs include:

- *Career Navigator*
- *Choices*
- *Discover*

- *Guidance Information System* (GIS)
- *Self-Directed Search (SDS) Form R*
- *SIGI-Plus*

Most of these programs do much more than just assess skills. They also integrate other key components in the career planning process – values, interests, goals, related jobs, college majors, education and training programs, and job search plans. These programs are widely available in schools, colleges, One-Stop Career Centers, and libraries across the country and many are free of charge in your community. You might check with the career or counseling center at your local community college or your local One-Stop Career Center (visit www.servicelocator.org and www.careeronestop.org for various locations) to see what computerized career assessment programs are available for your use.

Relatively easy to use and taking one to two hours to complete, these programs generate a great deal of valuable career and job information. Many will print out a useful analysis of how your interests and skills are related to specific jobs and careers. Such programs come closest to our notion of a magic bullet – they generate a great deal of personal and professional data for such a small investment of time, effort, and money.

Your Interests and Values

Just knowing your abilities and skills will not give your job search the direction it needs for finding a job that's right for you – one you both do well and enjoy doing. You also need to know your **work values and interests**. These are the basic building blocks for setting goals and targeting your abilities toward certain jobs and careers.

Take, for example, the ex-offender who does a superb job cleaning floors, hauling trash, or typing. While he possesses marketable skills (janitors, trash haulers, computer operators are in demand), if he doesn't regularly use these job-related skills and is more interested in working outdoors or with people, his abilities will not become **motivated skills**. In the end, your interests and values will determine which skills should play a central role in your job search.

Work, Leisure, and Home-Based Interests

We all have interests. Most change over time. Many of your interests may center on your past jobs, whereas others relate to activities that define your hobbies and leisure activities. Still other interests may relate to your dreams.

Examine the following list of interest areas. In the first column check those work areas that appeal to you. In the second column rank order those areas you checked in the first column. Start with "1" to indicate the most interesting:

Your Work Interests

Yes/No (x)	Ranking (1-12)	Interest Area
___	___	**Artistic:** An interest in creative expression of feelings or ideas.
___	___	**Scientific:** An interest in discovering, collecting, and analyzing information about the natural world, and in applying scientific research findings to problems in medicine, the life sciences, and the nature sciences.
___	___	**Plants and animals:** An interest in working with plants and animals, usually outdoors.
___	___	**Protective:** An interest in using authority to protect people and property.
___	___	**Mechanical:** An interest in applying mechanical principles to practical situations by using machines or hand tools.
___	___	**Industrial:** An interest in repetitive, concrete, organized activities done in a factory setting.
___	___	**Business detail:** An interest in organized, clearly defined activities requiring accuracy and attention to details (office settings).
___	___	**Selling:** An interest in bringing others to a particular point of view by personal persuasion, using sales and promotion techniques.
___	___	**Accommodating:** An interest in catering to the wishes and needs of others, usually on a one-to-one basis.
___	___	**Humanitarian:** An interest in helping others with their mental, spiritual, social, physical, or vocational needs.
___	___	**Leading and influencing:** An interest in leading and influencing others by using high-level verbal or numerical abilities.
___	___	**Physical performing:** An interest in physical activities performed before an audience.

You may discover that some of your home-based and leisure activity interests should become your work interests. Examples of such interests include:

Leisure and Home-Based Interests

___ Acting in a play or amateur variety show.
___ Advising family members on their personal problems.
___ Announcing or emceeing a program.
___ Applying first aid in emergencies as a volunteer.
___ Building model airplanes, automobiles, or boats.
___ Building or repairing radios, televisions, or other electronic equipment.
___ Buying large quantities of food or other products for an organization.
___ Campaigning for political candidates or issues.
___ Canning and preserving food.
___ Carving small wooden objects.
___ Coaching children or youth in sports activities.
___ Collecting experiments involving plants.
___ Conducting house-to-house or telephone surveys for a PTA or other organization.
___ Creating or styling hairdos for friends.
___ Designing your own greeting cards and writing original verses.

___ Developing film/printing pictures.
___ Doing impersonations.
___ Doing public speaking or debating.
___ Entertaining at parties or other events.
___ Helping conduct physical exercises for disabled people.
___ Making ceramic objects.
___ Modeling clothes for a fashion show.
___ Mounting and framing pictures.
___ Nursing sick pets.
___ Painting the interior or exterior of a home.
___ Playing a musical instrument.
___ Refinishing or re-upholstering furniture.
___ Repairing electrical household appliances.
___ Repairing the family car.
___ Repairing or assembling bicycles.
___ Repairing indoor plumbing.
___ Speaking on radio or television.
___ Taking photographs.
___ Teaching in Sunday School.
___ Tutoring pupils in school subjects.
___ Weaving rugs or making quilts.
___ Writing articles, stories, or plays.
___ Writing songs for club socials or amateur plays.

Indeed, many people turn hobbies or home activities into full-time jobs after deciding that such "work" is what they really enjoy doing.

Your Key Work Values

Work values are those things you like to do. They give you pleasure and enjoyment. Most jobs involve a combination of likes and dislikes. By identifying what you both like and dislike about jobs, you should be able to better identify jobs that involve tasks you most enjoy. Several exercises can help you identify your work values. First, identify what most satisfies you about work by completing this exercise:

My Work Values

I prefer employment which enables me to:

___ contribute to society	___ be creative
___ have contact with people	___ supervise others
___ work alone	___ work with details
___ work with a team	___ gain recognition
___ compete with others	___ acquire security
___ make decisions	___ make money
___ work under pressure	___ help others
___ use power and authority	___ solve problems
___ acquire new knowledge	___ take risks
___ be a recognized expert	___ work at own pace

Select four work values from the above list which are the most important to you and list them in the space below. List any other work values (desired satisfactions) which were not listed above but are nonetheless important to you:

1. _____

2. _____

3. _____

4. _____

If you feel you need to go beyond the above exercises, try this one. In the first column check those values that are most important to you. In the second column rank order the five most important values:

Ranking Work Values

Yes/No (x)	Ranking (1-5)	Work Values
____	____	**Adventure:** Working in a job that requires taking risks.
____	____	**Authority:** Working in a job in which you use your position to control others.
____	____	**Competition:** Working in a job in which you compete with others.
____	____	**Creativity and self-expression:** Working in a job in which you use your imagination to find new ways to do or say something.
____	____	**Flexible work schedule:** Working in a job in which you choose your hours to work.
____	____	**Helping others:** Working in a job in which you provide direct services to persons with problems.
____	____	**High salary:** Working in a job where many workers earn a large amount of money.
____	____	**Independence:** Working in a job in which you decide for yourself what work to do and how to do it.
____	____	**Influencing others:** Working in a job in which you influence the opinions of others or decisions of others.
____	____	**Intellectual stimulation:** Working in a job which requires a great amount of thought and reasoning.
____	____	**Leadership:** Working in a job in which you direct, manage, or supervise the activities of other people.
____	____	**Outside work:** Working out-of-doors.
____	____	**Persuading:** Working in a job in which you personally convince others to take certain actions.
____	____	**Physical work:** Working in a job which requires substantial physical activity.
____	____	**Prestige:** Working in a job which gives you status and respect in the community.
____	____	**Public attention:** Working in a job in which you attract immediate notice because of appearance or activity.

____ ____ **Public contact:** Working in a job dealing with the public.
____ ____ **Recognition:** Working in a job in which you gain public notice.
____ ____ **Research work:** Working in a job in which you search for and discover new facts and develop ways to apply them.
____ ____ **Routine work:** Working in a job in which you follow established procedures requiring little change.
____ ____ **Seasonal work:** Working in a job in which you are employed only at certain times of the year.
____ ____ **Travel:** Working in a job in which you take frequent trips.
____ ____ **Variety:** Working in a job in which your duties change frequently.
____ ____ **Work with children:** Working in a job in which you teach or care for children.
____ ____ **Work with hands:** Working in a job in which you use your hands or hand tools.
____ ____ **Work with machines or equipment:** Working in a job in which you use machines or equipment.
____ ____ **Work with numbers:** Working in a job in which you use mathematics or statistics.

Second, develop a comprehensive list of your past and present **job frustrations and dissatisfactions**. This should help you identify negative factors you should avoid in future jobs.

My Job Frustrations and Dissatisfactions

List as well as rank order as many past and present things that frustrate or make you dissatisfied and unhappy in job situations:

Rank

1. _____ ____
2. _____ ____
3. _____ ____
4. _____ ____
5. _____ ____
6. _____ ____
7. _____ ____
8. _____ ____
9. _____ ____
10. _____ ____

Third, brainstorm a list of "Ten or More Things I Love to Do." Identify which ones could be incorporated into what kinds of work environments:

Ten or More Things I Love To Do

Item	Related Work Environment
1. _____	_____
2. _____	_____
3. _____	_____
4. _____	_____
5. _____	_____
6. _____	_____
7. _____	_____
8. _____	_____
9. _____	_____
10. _____	_____

Fourth, list at least 10 things you most enjoy about work and rank each item accordingly:

Ten Things I Enjoy the Most About Work

	Rank
1. _____	_____
2. _____	_____
3. _____	_____
4. _____	_____
5. _____	_____
6. _____	_____
7. _____	_____
8. _____	_____
9. _____	_____
10. _____	_____

Fifth, you should also identify the types of interpersonal environments you prefer working in. Do this by specifying the types of people you like and dislike associating with:

Interpersonal Environments

Characteristics of people I like working with:	Characteristics of people I dislike working with:
_____	_____
_____	_____
_____	_____
_____	_____
_____	_____
_____	_____
_____	_____

No one test, instrument, or exercise will give you complete assessment information. You are well advised to use a variety of approaches to answer your self-assessment questions in the process of identifying what you really want to do.

Identify Your Motivated Abilities and Skills (MAS)

Once you know what you really do well and enjoy doing, your next task should be to analyze those interests, values, abilities, skills, and temperaments that form a **recurring motivated pattern**. This pattern is the single most important piece of information you need to know about yourself in the whole self-assessment process. Knowing your skills and abilities alone without understanding how they relate to your interests, values, and temperament will not give you the necessary direction for finding the job you want. You simply **must** know your pattern. Once you do, your job search activities may take on a whole new direction that will produce amazing results. You'll be able to state a clear objective (Chapter 8) that will guide you toward achieving your goals. So let's discover your pattern.

What's Your MAS?

Your pattern of motivated abilities and skills becomes evident once you analyze your **achievements or accomplishments**. For it is your achievements that tell us what you both do well and enjoy doing. If we looks at many of your achievements, we are likely to identify a **recurring pattern** that probably goes back to your childhood and which will continue to characterize your achievements in the future.

An equally useful exercise is to identify your **weaknesses** by identifying your bad habits and analyzing your failures. These, too, would fall into recurring patterns. Understanding what your weaknesses are might help you avoid jobs and work situations that bring out the worst rather than the best in you. Indeed, you may learn more about yourself by analyzing your failures than by focusing solely on your accomplishments.

Another interesting approach is to examine how you have dealt with some of life's most **challenging situations**, such as your incarceration, an illness, accident, divorce, financial difficulties, starting a business, or a death in the family. Many of these difficult situations required character, drive, persistence, and problem-solving strategies beyond the ordinary. They may have drawn on inner strengths or a reservoir of skills you never knew you had but which occasionally came to the forefront when you were under extreme pressure. Moreover, your handling of these difficult situations might have led to life-altering consequences for you and those around you.

For now, let's focus on your positives rather than identify your negatives or how you coped with difficult situations. After you complete the strength exercises, you may want to reverse the procedures to identify your weaknesses and challenges.

Numerous self-directed exercises can assist you in identifying your pattern of motivated abilities and skills. The basic requirements for making these exercises work for you are **time and analytical ability**. You must spend a great deal of time detailing your achievements by examining your history of accomplishments. Once you complete the historical reconstruction task, you must comb through your "stories" to identify **recurring** themes and patterns. This requires a high level of analytical ability which you may or may not possess. If analysis and synthesis are not two of your strong skills, you may want to seek assistance from someone who is good at analyzing and synthesizing information presented in narrative form.

Motivated Skills Exercise

One of the most useful exercises we and thousands of others use yields some of the best data on motivated abilities and skills. This exercise helps you identify which skills you **enjoy** using. While you can do it on your own, it is best to work with someone else. Since you will need six to eight hours to properly complete this exercise, divide your time into two or three work sessions.

The exercise consists of six steps. The steps follow the basic pattern of generating raw data, identifying patterns, analyzing the data through reduction techniques, and synthesizing the patterns into a transferable skills vocabulary. You need strong analytical skills to complete this exercise on your own. The six steps include:

1. **Identify 15-20 achievements:** While ideally you should inventory over 100-150 achievements, let's start by focusing on a minimum of 15-20 achievements. These consist of things you enjoyed doing, believe you did well, and felt a sense of satisfaction, pride, or accomplishment in doing. You can see yourself performing at your best and enjoying your experiences when you analyze your achievements. This information reveals your motivations since it deals entirely with your voluntary behavior. In addition, it identifies what is right with you by focusing on your positives and strengths. Identify achieve-ments throughout your life, beginning with your childhood. Your achievements should relate to specific experiences – not general ones – and may be drawn from work, leisure, education, military, prison, or home life. Put each achieve-ment at the top of a separate sheet of paper on which you will further elaborate. For example, your achievements might appear as follows:

Sample Achievement Statements

"When I was 10 years old, I started a small paper route and built it up to the largest in my district."

_____

"I started playing basketball in ninth grade and became team captain in my junior year, the same year we had an undefeated season."

_____

"When I was in junior high school, I sang tenor in the church choir and was asked to sing solos at several Sunday services."

_____

"Designed, constructed, and displayed the Christmas nativity display at my church when I was 16 years old."

_____

"Earned enough money as a cook at Jerry's Diner to help my grandmother buy a much-needed pair of eyeglasses."

_____

"While I was small compared to other guys, I made the first string on my high school football team."

_____

"Although incarcerated and struggling with reading, I was the first in my family to complete a GED and start working on a college degree."

_____

"I helped a fellow inmate improve his reading and persuaded him to complete his GED and participate in the vocational program. I was so proud to learn he got a job three weeks after release and is now doing very well and has even enrolled in junior college."

_____

"I proposed reorganizing the prison library and was put in charge of a team of four people who developed and implemented a plan that resulted in a 15-percent increase in the use of the library by fellow inmates. The warden complimented me on my excellent work."

_____

2. Prioritize your seven most significant achievements.

1. _____

2. _____

3. _____

4. _____

5. _____

6. _____

7. _____

3. **Write a full page on each of your prioritized achievements.** You should describe:

- How you initially became involved.
- The details of **what you did** and **how you did it.**
- What was especially enjoyable or satisfying to you.

Use copies of the "Detailing Your Achievements" form on page 63 to outline your achievements.

4. **Elaborate on your achievements:** Have one or two other people interview you. For each achievement have them note on a separate sheet of paper any terms used to reveal your skills, abilities, and personal qualities. To elaborate details, the interviewer(s) may ask:

- What was involved in the achievement?
- What was your part?
- What did you actually do?
- How did you go about that?

Clarify any vague areas by providing an example or illustration of what you actually did. Use these questions to get more details:

- Would you describe in detail one example of what you mean?
- Could you give me an illustration?
- What were you good at doing?

This interview should clarify the details of your activities by asking only "what" and "how" questions. It should take 45 to 90 minutes to complete. Make copies of the "Strength Identification Interview" form on page 64 to guide you through this interview.

5. **Identify patterns by examining the interviewer's notes:** Together, identify the recurring skills, abilities, and personal qualities **demonstrated** in your achievements. Search for patterns. Your skills pattern should be clear at this point; you should feel comfortable with it. If you have questions, review the data. If you disagree with a conclusion, disregard it. The results must accurately and honestly reflect how you operate.

Detailing Your Achievements

ACHIEVEMENT # ___: _____

_____

_____

1. How did I initially become involved? _____

_____

_____

_____

2. What did I do? _____

_____

_____

_____

_____

3. How did I do it? _____

_____

_____

_____

_____

4. What was especially enjoyable about doing it?

_____

_____

_____

_____

Strength Identification Interview

Interviewee _____   Interviewer _____

INSTRUCTIONS: For each achievement experience, identify the **skills** and **abilities** the achiever actually demonstrated. Obtain details of the experience by asking **what** was involved with the achievement and **how** the individual made the achievement happen. Avoid "why" questions which tend to mislead. Ask for examples or illustrations of **what** and **how**.

Achievement #1:

Achievement #2:

Achievement #3:

Recurring abilities and skills:

6. **Synthesize the information by clustering similar skills into categories:** For example, your skills might be grouped in the following manner:

Synthesized Skill Clusters

Investigate/Survey/Read   Teach/Train/Drill
Inquire/Probe/Question   Perform/Show/Demonstrate

Learn/Memorize/Practice   Construct/Assemble/Put together
Evaluate/Appraise/Assess
Compare   Organize/Structure/Provide
                                 definition/Plan/Chart course
Influence/Involve/Get   Strategize/Coordinate
participation/Publicize
Promote   Create/Design/Adapt/Modify

This exercise yields a relatively comprehensive inventory of your skills. The information will better enable you to use a **skills vocabulary** when identifying your objective,
writing your resume and letters, and interviewing. If you are like many others who have
successfully completed this exercise, your self-confidence and self-esteem should increase
accordingly.

Become a Purpose-Driven Ex-Offender

All of the exercises outlined in this chapter were designed to explore your **past** and
present. At the same time, you need to project your skills and values into the **future**.
What, for example, do you want to do over the next 10 to 20 years? We examine this
question in the next chapter when we focus on developing a powerful objective for guiding
your job search and perhaps your life.

Once you formulate your objective, you'll be prepared to take action that should lead
to a good job. Highly motivated and focused, you'll organize an effective job search that
focuses laser-like on what you do well and enjoy doing. With an objective clearly reflecting
your skills and values, a whole new world of work and satisfaction will open to you. You
will become a purpose-driven ex-offender who knows exactly what he or she wants to do,
and you'll become single-minded in achieving your goal.

As we noted earlier, you have power within you to change your life. Unleashing that
power requires relating all of the information you gathered on yourself in this chapter,
especially your MAS, to the important work you will do in the next chapter to develop
that all-important objective.

8

Develop a Powerful Objective

G OALS AND OBJECTIVES ARE STATEMENTS of what you want to do in the future. When combined with your interests, values, abilities, and skills, and related to specific jobs, they give your job search needed direction and meaning for the purpose of targeting specific employers. Without them, your job search may become disorganized as you present an image of uncertainty and confusion to potential employers.

Employers want to hire talented, enthusiastic, and purposeful individuals. Your goal should be to find a job or career that is compatible with your interests, motivations, skills, and talents as well as related to a vision of your future. In other words, **try to find a job fit for you and your future rather than try to fit into a job that happens to be advertised** and for which you think you might qualify. Your ultimate goal should be to find a job and career you really love.

Focus On Employers' Needs

Your objective should be a concise statement of what you want to do and what you have to offer to an employer. The position you seek is "what you want to do"; your qualifications are "what you have to offer."

Your objective should state your strongest qualifications for meeting employers' needs. It should communicate what you have to offer an employer without emphasizing what you expect the employer to do for you. In other words, your objective should be **work-centered**, not self-centered; it should not contain over-used terms that emphasize what **you** want, such as give me a(n) "opportunity for advancement," "position working with people," "progressive company," or "creative position." Such terms are viewed today as "canned" job search language which say little of value about you, the candidate. Above all, your objective should reflect your honesty and integrity; it should not be "hyped."

Project Yourself Into the Future

Even after identifying your abilities and skills, specifying an **objective** can be the most difficult and tedious step in the job search process; it can stall the resume writing process indefinitely. This simple one-sentence, 25-word statement can take days or weeks to formulate and clearly define. Yet, it must be specified prior to writing the resume and engaging in other job search steps. An objective gives meaning and direction to all other activities in your job search.

Four major steps are involved in developing a realistic work objective. Each step can be implemented in a variety of ways:

STEP 1: Develop or obtain basic information on your functional/transfer-able skills, which we discussed in Chapter 7.

STEP 2: Acquire supportive information about yourself from others, tests, and yourself. Several resources are available for this purpose:

A. **From others:** Ask three to five individuals whom you know well, and whose opinions are likely to be similar to employers, to evaluate you according to the questions in the "Strength Evaluation" form on page 68. Explain to these people that you believe their candid opinion will help you better understand of your strengths and weaknesses from the perspectives of others. Make copies of this form and ask your evaluators to complete and return it to a designated third party who will share the information – but not the respondent's name – with you.

B. **From vocational tests:** Although we prefer self-generated data, vocationally oriented tests can help clarify, confirm, and translate your understanding of yourself into occupational directions. If you decide to use vocational tests, contact a professional career counselor who can administer and interpret the tests. We recommend taking the following tests:

- *Myers-Briggs Type Indicator®*
- *Strong Interest Inventory®*
- *Self-Directed Search (SDS)®*

C. **From yourself:** Refer to the previous exercises in Chapter 7 that assist you in identifying your work values, job frustrations and dissatisfactions, things you love to do, things you enjoy most about work, and your preferred interpersonal environments.

Strength Evaluation

TO: _____

FROM: _____

I am going through a career assessment process and thought you would be an appropriate person to ask for assistance. Would you please truthfully respond to the questions below? Your comments will be given to me by the individual named below; s/he will not reveal your name. Your comments will be used for advising purposes only. Thank you.

What are my strengths?

What weak areas might I need to improve?

In your opinion, what do I need in a job or career to make me satisfied?

Please return to: _____

STEP 3: Project your values and preferences into the future by completing simulation and creative thinking exercises:

A. **Ten Million Dollar Exercise:** First, assume that you are given a $10,000,000 gift; now you don't have to work. Since the gift is restricted to your use only, you cannot give any part of it away. What will you do with your time? At first? Later on? Second, assume that you are given another $10,000,000, but this time you are required to give it all away. What kinds of causes, organizations, charities, etc. would you support? Complete the following form in which you answer these questions:

What Will I Do With Two $10,000,000?

First gift is restricted to my use only:

_____

_____

_____

Second gift must be given away:

_____

_____

_____

B. **Obituary Exercise:** Make a list of the most important things you would like to do or accomplish before you die. Two alternatives are available for doing this. First, make a list in response to this lead-in statement: *"Before I die, I want to..."*

Before I Die, I Want to . . .

1. _____

_____

2. _____

_____

3. _____

_____

4. _____

_____

5. _____

_____

Second, write a newspaper article which is your hypothetical obituary for 10 years from now. Stress your accomplishments over the coming 10-year period.

My Obituary

Obituary for Mr./Ms. _____ to appear in the _____
_____ Newspaper in the year 20_____.

_____

_____

_____

_____

_____

_____

_____

_____

_____

_____

_____

_____

_____

C. My Ideal Work Week: Starting with Monday, place each day of the week as the headings of seven sheets of paper. Develop a daily calendar with 30-minute intervals, beginning at 7am and ending at midnight. Your calendar should consist of a 118-hour week. Next, beginning at 7am on Monday (sheet one), identify the **ideal activities** you would enjoy doing, or need to do, for each 30-minute segment during the day. Assume you are capable of doing anything; you have no requirements except those you impose on yourself. Furthermore, assume that your work schedule consists of 40 hours per week. How will you fill your time? Be specific.

D. My Ideal Job Description: Develop your ideal future job. Be sure you include:

- Specific interests you want to build into your job
- Work responsibilities
- Working conditions
- Earnings and benefits

- Interpersonal environment
- Working circumstances, opportunities, and goals

Description of My Ideal Job

_____

_____

_____

_____

_____

_____

_____

_____

_____

_____

_____

_____

_____

_____

_____

_____

STEP 4: Test your objective against reality. Evaluate and refine it by doing the following:

A. Market Research: Four steps are involved in conducting market research:

1. Products or services: Based upon all other assessment activities, make a list of what you **do** or **make**:

Products/Services I Do or Make

1. _____

2. _____

3. _____

4. _____

5. _____

6. _____

7. _____

8. _____

2. **Market:** Identify who needs, wants, or buys what you do or make. Be very specific. Include individuals, groups, and organizations. Then, identify **what** specific **needs** your products or services fill. Next, assess the **results** you achieve with your products or services.

The Market for My Products/Services

Individuals, groups, and organizations needing me:

1. _____

2. _____

3. _____

4. _____

Needs I fulfill:

1. _____

2. _____

3. _____

4. _____

Results/outcomes/impacts of my products/services:

1. _____

2. _____

3. _____

4. _____

3. **New Markets:** Brainstorm a list of **who else** needs your products or services. Think about ways of expanding your market. Next, list any new needs your current or new market has which you might be able to fill:

Developing New Needs

Who else needs my products/services?

1. _____

2. _____

3. _____

4. _____

New ways to expand my market:

1. _____

2. _____

3. _____

4. _____

New needs I should fulfill:

1. _____

2. _____

3. _____

4. _____

4. **New products and/or services:** List any new products or services you can offer and any new needs you can satisfy:

New Products/Services I Can Offer

1. _____

2. _____

3. _____

4. _____

New Needs I Can Meet

1. _____

2. _____

3. _____

4. _____

B. **Force Field Analysis:** Once you develop a tentative or firm objective, force field analysis can help you understand the various internal and external forces affecting the achievement of your objective. You complete force field analysis by engaging in the following order of activities:

- **Clearly state your objective or course of action.** Make sure it's based upon your MAS from Chapter 7 and is employer-oriented rather than self-centered.

- **List the positive and negative forces affecting your objective.** Specify the internal and external forces working **for** and **against** you in terms of who, what, where, when, and how much. Estimate the impact of each on your objective.

- **Analyze the forces.** Assess the importance of each force upon your objective and its probable effect upon you. Some forces may be irrelevant to your goal. You may need additional information to make a thorough analysis.

- **Maximize positive forces and minimize negative ones.** Identify actions you can take to strengthen positive forces and to neutralize, overcome, or reverse negative forces. Focus on real, important, and probable key forces.

- **Assess the likelihood of attaining your objective** and, if necessary, modify it in light of new information.

C. **Conduct Online and Library Research:** This research should strengthen and clarify your objective. Consult various reference materials on alternative jobs – most are available at your local library or bookstore. Some are available electronically and can be accessed through your local library. (Check to see if your library has online databases, such as Dun and Bradstreet's, which can be accessed from a home computer.) If you explore the numerous company profiles and career sites available on the Internet, you should be able to tap into a wealth of information on alternative jobs and careers. Two good resources for beginning online research are Margaret Riley Dikel's *The Guide to Internet Job Search* (McGraw-Hill) and Ron and Caryl Krannich, *America's Top Internet Job Sites* (Impact Publications). See Chapter 9 for more information on conducting research.

D. **Conduct Informational Interviews:** This may be the most useful way to clarify and refine your objective. See Chapter 11 for details on networking and informational interviews.

Your work objective is a function of both subjective and objective information and a combination of idealism and realism. We believe the strongest emphasis should be placed on your competencies and should include as much information on yourself as possible. Your work objective is realistic in that it is tempered by your past experiences, accomplishments, skills, and current research. An objective formulated in this manner permits you to think beyond your past experiences – a definite plus for ex-offenders who need to chart a new life after prison.

State a Functional Objective

Your job objective should be oriented toward skills and results or outcomes. You can begin by stating a functional job objective at two different levels: a general objective and a specific one for communicating your qualifications to employers both on resumes and in interviews. Thus, this objective-setting process sets the stage for other key job search activities. For the general objective, begin with the statement:

Stating Your General Objective

I would like a job where I can use my ability to _____
which will result in _____.

The objective in this statement is both a **skill** and an **outcome**. For example, you might state:

Skills-Based and Results-Oriented Objective

I would like a job where my experience in landscaping, supported by strong design interests and maintenance abilities, will result in more customers and greater profits for the company.

At a second level you may wish to re-write this objective in order to target it at various landscaping companies. For example, on your resume it could become:

Job-Targeted Objective

An increasingly responsible planning position in landscaping, where proven design and maintenance abilities will be used for expanding the company's clientele.

The following are examples of weak and strong objective statements. Various styles are also presented.

Weak Objectives

A challenging Landscaping position with a progressive company that leads to career advancement.

_____

A position in Substance Abuse Counseling that will allow me to work with people in a helping capacity.

_____

A position in Electronics with a progressive firm.

_____

Sales Representative with opportunity for advancement.

_____

Stronger Objectives

*To use computer science training in **software development** for designing and implementing operating systems.*

_____

*To use innovative **landscape design** training for developing award-winning approaches to designing commercial properties.*

_____

*A responsible **front desk position** with a major hotel that uses strong organization and communication skills for improving customer service.*

---

*A **masonry position** with a commercial construction firm that values creative stonework and rewards hard working, responsible, and loyal employees.*

---

*A challenging **sales position** in real estate where sales/customer service experience and strong communication and market skills will be used for expanding agency listings and commercial sales. Long term goal: top sales associate within five years and general manager of a branch real estate office within 10 years.*

It is important to relate your objective to your audience. While you definitely want a good job that pays well, your audience wants to know what you can do for them in exchange for a good paying job. Remember, your objective should be work-centered, not self-centered.

Based on the above discussion and examples, state your job objective:

My Job Objective

_____

_____

_____

_____

Now look at the job objective you have written and try to make it stronger. Does it state your skill(s) related to the job? Does it say what you can/will do for the employer?

_____

_____

_____

Your objective will become the key element for organizing all other elements on your resume. It gives meaning and direction to your job search. Your objective says something very important about how you want to conduct your life with the employer. It gives them an important indicator of the **value** you will bring to this job. Most important of all, it tells them who you really are in terms of your key values and accomplishments – a short answer to the big question of *"Why should I hire you?"*

9

Conduct Research on Jobs, Employers, and Communities

S INCE YOU MAY KNOW LITTLE about the job market, you need to acquire information in several important employment areas. These should become the central focus of your research activities:

1. **Job alternatives:** What jobs are available and which ones most interest you? What are the education and skill requirements, working conditions, and potential salary, benefits, and advancement opportunities?

2. **Employers and companies:** Who's hiring for what types of jobs? How do you reach the people who make the hiring decisions?

3. **Communities and neighborhoods:** Are you looking in the right places? Will you need to move or commute to your next job? Do you have probation or parole issues that may prevent you from relocating to another community?

Much research can be done during your pre-release. You can visit your library for resources, talk to correctional staff members, and write letters to family members, friends, and potential employers. If you do nothing else while incarcerated, read, read, read, and write, write, write about alternative jobs, employers, and communities. Talk to people in your institution about possible jobs and careers. Get focused on your future and develop new goals (Chapter 8). Learn to conduct informational interviews (see Chapter 11), which lead to acquiring information, advice, and referrals, by communicating with knowledgeable people.

Once you are released, your research options will increase dramatically. Now you can work with your P.O., who may have a list of local employers who regularly hire ex-offenders, and visit your local library, One-Stop Career Center, and several support groups that assist ex-offenders in transition. You can use the Internet and interview people by phone, e-mail, and in face-to-face meetings. Use these resources frequently. Start developing a plan of action for creating a new future centered around goals and employment.

Job Alternatives

If you don't know what you want to do, you should do research on alternative jobs and careers. The following books, which are available in many libraries and bookstores, will help you survey various alternatives relevant to the interests, skills, and educational backgrounds of ex-offenders:

- *25 Jobs That Have It All*
- *50 Best Jobs for Your Personality*
- *250 Best Jobs Through Apprenticeships*
- *300 Best Jobs Without a Four-Year Degree*
- *America's Top 100 Jobs for People Without a Four-Year Degree*
- *America's Top Jobs for People Re-Entering the Workforce*
- *America's Top 101 Computer Technical Jobs*
- *Career Guide to America's Top Industries*
- *Careers in Travel, Tourism, and Hospitality*
- *Cool Careers for Dummies*
- *Enhanced Occupational Outlook Handbook*
- *Entry-Level Jobs*
- *Great Jobs in Two Years*
- *High-Tech Careers for Low-Tech People*
- *Occupational Outlook Handbook*
- *The O*NET Dictionary of Occupational Titles*
- *Outdoor Careers*
- *Quick Guide to Career Training in Two Years or Less*
- *Quick Prep Careers*
- *Top 100 Health Care Careers*

We especially recommend reviewing the U.S. Department of Labor's *Occupational Outlook Handbook* and *The O*NET Dictionary of Occupational Titles*. Both books also can be viewed online by visiting these two websites:

- *Occupational Outlook Handbook*   www.bls.gov/oco
- *The O*NET Dictionary*   www.onetcenter.org

The *Occupational Outlook Handbook* reviews nearly 300 occupations covering over 85 percent of all jobs. *The O*NET Dictionary of Occupational Titles* provides details on nearly 1,110 jobs.

The U.S. Department of Labor gathers a great deal of information on growing and declining jobs. For example, recent surveys indicate the following jobs are the fastest growing jobs in the decade ahead. Each requires particular levels of education and training. As might be expected in today's high-tech and service economy, technical and service occupations will grow the fastest in the coming decade:

Fastest Growing Occupations, 2002-2012
(Numbers in thousands of jobs)

Occupational Title	Employment 2002	Employment 2012	Percent Change	Postsecondary Education or Training Needed
Medical assistants [3]	365	579	59	Moderate-term on-the-job training
Network systems and data communications analysts [1]	186	292	57	Bachelor's degree
Physician assistants [3]	63	94	49	Bachelor's degree
Social and human service assistants [3]	305	454	49	Moderate-term on-the-job training
Home health aides [4]	580	859	48	Short-term on-the-job training
Medical records and health information technicians [3]	147	216	47	Associate degree
Physical therapist aides [3]	37	54	46	Short-term on-the-job training
Computer software engineers, applications [1]	394	573	46	Bachelor's degree
Computer software engineers [1]	281	409	45	Bachelor's degree
Physical therapist assistants [2]	50	73	45	Associate degree
Fitness trainers and aerobics instructors [3]	183	264	44	Postsecondary vocational award
Database administrators [1]	110	159	44	Bachelor's degree
Veterinary technologists and technicians [3]	53	76	44	Associate degree
Hazardous materials removal workers [2]	38	54	43	Moderate-term on-the-job training
Dental hygienists [1]	148	212	43	Associate degree
Occupational therapist aides [3]	8	12	43	Short-term on-the-job training
Dental assistants [3]	266	379	42	Moderate-term on-the-job training
Personal and home care aides [4]	608	854	40	Short-term on-the-job training
Self-enrichment education teachers [2]	200	281	40	Work experience in a related occupation
Computer systems analysts [1]	468	653	39	Bachelor's degree
Occupational therapist assistants [2]	18	26	39	Associate degree
Environmental engineers [1]	47	65	38	Bachelor's degree
Postsecondary teachers [1]	1,581	1,284	38	Doctoral degree
Network and computer systems administrators [1]	251	345	37	Bachelor's degree
Environmental science and protection technicians, including health [2]	28	38	37	Associate degree
Preschool teachers, except special education [4]	424	577	36	Postsecondary vocational award
Computer and information systems managers [1]	284	387	36	Bachelor's or higher degree, plus Work experience
Physical therapists [1]	137	185	35	Master's degree
Occupational therapists [1]	82	110	35	Bachelor's degree
Respiratory therapists [2]	86	116	35	Associate degree

[1] Very high average annual earnings ($42,820 and over)
[2] High average annual earnings ($27,500 to $41,780)
[3] Low average annual earnings ($19,710 to $27,380)
[4] Very low average annual earnings (up to $19,600)

Employers and Companies

While it's important to know about alternative jobs and careers, including growing and declining occupations, in the end, you need information on who is actually hiring for what types of jobs in **your** community. Be sure to visit your local library and One-Stop Career Center, which will have a great deal of information on local businesses and employers. Ask for assistance in locating employers. The One-Stop Career Center may have a series of notebooks on local companies, including current job listings provided by various employers.

One of your best sources of information on employers and companies will be the Internet. Most businesses and organizations have their own websites, which include information about what they do and who and how they hire. Many also will have online application forms or information on submitting an electronic resume. You can easily find employers by using any major search engine, such as Google.com, Yahoo.com, MSN.com, or AskJeeves.com. Our favorite gateway websites or online directories to businesses and companies include:

■ CEO Express	www.ceoexpress.com
■ Hoover's Online	www.hoovers.com
■ Dun and Bradstreet's Million Dollar Databases	www.dnbmdd.com/mddi
■ Corporate Information	www.corporateinformation.com
■ BizTech Network	www.brint.com

Individuals interested in working for nonprofit organizations should visit these useful websites:

■ GuideStar	www.guidestar.org
■ Action Without Borders	www.idealist.org
■ Foundation Center	www.fdncenter.org
■ Independent Sector	www.independentsector.org

Communities

If the terms of your release (probation, parole, or the nature of your crime) involve community restrictions, or if you lack appropriate education and marketable skills for today's job market, this section may be of limited usefulness.

Research on different communities can be initiated from your local library or on a computer connected to the Internet. Several resources will provide you with a current profile of various communities. Many libraries have a reference section of telephone books on various cities. If this section is weak or absent in your local library, check out several websites that function as **telephone directories**, such as:

■ Switchboard	www.switchboard.com
■ SuperPages	www.superpages.com
■ WhitePages	www.whitepages.com
■ Yellow Pages	www.yellow.com
■ Yahoo! Yellow Pages	http://yp.yahoo.com

In addition to giving you names, addresses, and telephone numbers, the Yellow Pages are invaluable sources of information on local companies and organizations.

Many large libraries also have state and community directories as well as subscriptions to some state and community magazines and city newspapers. Using the Internet, you can explore hundreds of **newspapers and magazines** linked to these key websites:

- **Internet Public Library**   www.ipl.org/div/news
- **NewsDirectory.com**   http://newsdirectory.com
- **Newslink**   http://newslink.org
- **Newspapers.com**   www.newspapers.com

Research magazine, journal, and newspaper articles on different communities by consulting several print and online references available through your local library.

The Internet has a wealth of information on the best places to live and work. Start with these websites:

- **Find Your Spot**   www.findyourspot.com
- **Kid Friendly Cities**   www.kidfriendlycities.org
- **Sperling's BestPlaces**   www.bestplaces.net

For information on the **best places to work**, check out these websites:

- **EmploymentSpot**   www.employmentspot.com/lists
- **Fortune Magazine**   www.fortune.com (see "Rankings")
- **Great Place to Work**   http://greatplacetowork.com
- **JobStar Central**   www.jobstar.org/hidden/bestcos.htm

If you want to **explore various communities**, you should examine several of these gateway community sites:

- **AOL CityGuide**   http://digitalcity.com
- **Boulevards**   http://boulevards.com
- **Cities.com**   www.cities.com
- **CityGuides.Yahoo**   http://cityguides.local.yahoo.com

Several relocation websites also provide a wealth of information on communities. Check these sites out for **linkages to major communities**:

- **Homestore.com**   http://homestore.com
- **Monstermoving.com**   www.monstermoving.monster.com
- **Relocation Central**   http://relocationcentral.com

Most major communities and newspapers have websites. You'll find community-based information and linkages on such homepages, from newspapers and housing information to local employers, schools, recreation, and community services. Several employment sites include relocation information and salary calculators which provide information on the cost of living in, as well as the cost of moving to, different communities.

You should also consult several city job banks that will give you contact information on specific employers in major metropolitan communities. Adams Media regularly publishes *The National JobBank* as well as several annual job bank guides. Some of the most popular titles include:

- *Atlanta JobBank*
- *Austin/San Antonio JobBank*
- *Boston JobBank*
- *Carolina JobBank*
- *Colorado JobBank*
- *Chicago JobBank*
- *Dallas/Fort Worth JobBank*
- *Houston JobBank*
- *Los Angeles JobBank*
- *New Jersey JobBank*
- *New York JobBank*
- *Ohio JobBank*
- *Philadelphia JobBank*
- *Phoenix JobBank*
- *San Francisco JobBank*
- *Seattle JobBank*
- *Virginia JobBank*
- *Washington D.C. JobBank*

Questions You Should Ask

The key to conducting useful research lies in the questions you ask. Once you narrow your focus to a few companies and organizations, you should focus on three key questions that will yield useful information for guiding your job search:

- **Who has the power to hire?** It's seldom the personnel office, which is charged with administrative duties. Hiring power usually lies in the operating units – head of the unit you would be working in on a day-to-day basis. This question leads to several other related questions: Who describes the positions? Who announces vacancies? Who receives applications? Who administers tests? Who selects eligible candidates? Who chooses whom to interview? Who conducts the interview? Who offers the jobs?

- **How does the company or organization operate?** Try to learn as much as possible about internal operations. Is this a good place to work? Are employees generally happy working here? What about advancement opportunities, working conditions, relationships among co-workers and supervisors, growth patterns, internal politics, management style, work values, and opportunities for taking initiative?

- **What do I need to do to get a job with this company or organization?** The best way to find how to get a job in a particular organization is to follow the advice in Chapter 11 on prospecting, networking, and informational interviewing. This question can only be answered by talking to people who know both the formal and informal hiring practices. Your networking activities also will help you answer the first two questions.

As you can answer these questions, you'll learn at great deal about a potential employer. You'll discover whether or not you are interested in working for the company, and you'll acquire valuable inside information that will give you an edge over the competition. You'll know who should get your resume, and you'll be able to ask good questions at the job interview.

10

Write Effective Applications, Resumes, and Letters

EXCEPT FOR JOB SEEKERS WHO JUST show up (see pages 41-42), most employers want to see you on paper **before** they meet you in person. How you complete applications and write, produce, distribute, and follow up resumes and letters will largely determine whether or not you will be invited to a job interview and offered a job. As you will quickly discover, applications and resumes are **calling cards** for opening the doors of employers. Letters add sizzle to resumes as well as open more doors to getting a job. For more information on these subjects, see Wendy Enelow and Ron Krannich, *Best Resumes and Letters for Ex-Offenders* (Impact Publications, 2006)

Application Tips

Many employers require applicants to fill out job applications. If, for example, you walk into a grocery store or retail business, you may be asked to go to a computer screen, or kiosk, to complete an online application, or you will be given a two- to four-page application form to be completed by hand. Many companies routinely give anyone interested in a job a chance to fill out an application. The following 20 tips should help you best complete a job application and improve your chances of getting a job interview:

1. Dress neatly.
2. Take two copies of the application form.
3. Read the instructions carefully and follow them completely.
4. Use a black ink pen when writing.
5. Answer each question.
6. Try to write as neatly as possible.
7. Be prepared to complete each section of the application.
8. Include all previous employers.
9. If you lack work experience, be creative.
10. Appear educated, even if you lack formal credentials.
11. Handle sensitive questions with tact.
12. Avoid abbreviations.
13. Avoid vague statements.

14. Avoid revealing salary information.
15. Include interests and hobbies relevant to the job.
16. Include additional comments if appropriate.
17. Remember to sign the application.
18. Read and re-read your answers.
19. Attach your resume to the application form.
20. Be sure to follow up.

Resume Rules

Resumes play a central role in a job search. From the perspective of the employer, a resume should be a concise summary of your qualifications. It should reveal what you have done, can do, and are likely to do in the future. Employers use resumes to screen candidates both before and during interviews. During the interview, the information on the resume may be the subject of several questions about a candidate's background, accomplishments, and future goals.

From the perspective of job seekers, a resume is an **advertisement** for a job. Within the space of one or two pages, it should give just enough information to persuade the reader to interview the writer. It should:

- Clearly relate your purpose and competencies to employers' needs.
- Be concise and easy to read.
- Outline a pattern of success highlighted with examples of accomplishments.
- Motivate the reader to read it in-depth.
- Tell employers that you are a responsible and purposeful individual – a doer who can quickly solve their problems.

Keep in mind that most employers are busy people who normally glance at a resume for only 20 to 30 seconds. It must quickly motivate the reader to take action. Ask yourself this employer-centered question: *"What can this candidate do for me?"* Your answer should result in an attractive, interesting, unique, and skills-based resume.

Types of Resumes

You have four basic types of resumes to choose from: chronological, functional, combination, or resume letter. Each form has various advantages and disadvantages.

The **chronological resume** is the standard resume used by most applicants. It often comes in two forms: traditional and improved. The **traditional chronological resume** is also known as the "obituary resume," because it both "kills" your chances of getting a job and is a good source for writing your obituary. Primarily summarizing your work history, this resume lists dates and names first and duties and responsibilities second; it includes extraneous information such as height, weight, age, marital status, gender, and hobbies. While relatively easy to write, this is the most ineffective resume you can produce. Its purpose at best is to inform people of what you have done in the past as well as where, when, and with whom. It tells employers little or nothing about what you want to do, can do, and will do for them.

The **improved chronological resume** better communicates to employers your purpose, past achievements, and probable future performance. This resume works best for individuals who have extensive experience directly related to a position. This resume should include a clear work objective. The work experience section should include the names and locations of former employers followed by a brief description of major skills and accomplishments; employment dates should appear at the end. It should stress **accomplishments** and **skills** rather than formal duties and responsibilities – that you are a productive and responsible person who gets things done, a doer. While this resume performs better than the traditional chronological resume, it simply doesn't highlight very well major accomplishments and a pattern of success. Also, since you have an employment gap because of your incarceration, a chronological resume will draw attention to that gap.

Functional resumes should be used by individuals making a significant career change, first entering the workforce, or re-entering the job market after a lengthy absence. This resume should stress your accomplishments and transferable skills regardless of previous work settings and job titles. This could include accomplishments as a volunteer worker or member of an organization or group. Names of employers and dates of employment should not appear on this resume.

Functional resumes have certain weaknesses. Since many employers still look for names, dates, and direct job experience, this resume does not meet their expectations. You should use a functional resume if you have limited work experience or your past experience doesn't strengthen your new career objective. For many ex-offenders, this resume helps them deal with such issues as limited work experience and obvious time gaps.

Combination resumes, also known as hybrid resumes, combine the best features of both chronological and functional resumes. They stress accomplishments and skills as well as include work experience. This is the perfect resume for someone with work experience who wishes to change to a job in a related career field.

Resume letters substitute for resumes. Appearing as a job inquiry or application letter, resume letters highlight various sections of your resume, such as work history, experience, areas of effectiveness, objective, or education, in relation to employers' needs. These letters are used when you prefer not sending your more general resume. Resume letters have one major weakness: they give employers insufficient information and thus may prematurely eliminate you from consideration.

Structuring Resume Content

After choosing an appropriate resume format, you should generate the necessary information for structuring each category of your resume. You developed much of this information when you identified your motivated abilities and skills and specified your objective in Chapter 8. Include the following information on separate sheets of paper:

Contact Information:	Name, street address, and telephone/fax numbers, e-mail address.
Work Objective:	Refer to the information in Chapter 8 on writing an objective. If you completed this chapter properly, you formulated your job objective on page 76.
Education:	Degrees, schools, dates, highlights, special training.
Work Experience:	Paid, unpaid, civilian, military, and part-time employment. Include job titles, employers, locations, dates, skills, accomplishments, duties, and responsibilities. Use the functional language outlined on pages 50-51.

Achievements:	Things you did that **benefitted** others, especially initiatives that resulted in outcomes for employers.
Other Experience:	Volunteer, civic, and professional memberships. Include your contributions, demonstrated skills, offices held, names, and dates.
Special Skills or Licenses/Certificates	Computer, Internet, foreign languages, teaching, paramedical, etc. relevant to your objective.
Other Information:	References, expected salary, willingness to relocate/travel, availability dates, and other information supporting your objective.

Producing Drafts

Your next task is to include this information about yourself in draft resumes. If, for example, you write a combination resume (see page 91), your resume should be organized as follows:

- Contact information
- Work objective
- Qualifications/experience/achievements
- Work history or employment
- Education

Be careful in including any other type of information on your resume. Other information may distract from rather than strengthen your objective.

While your first draft may run more than two pages, try to get everything into one or two pages for the final draft. Most employers lose interest after reading the first page.

Resumes "Do's" and "Don'ts"

Your final resume draft should conform to the following rules for writing a great resume:

Resume "Don'ts"

- **Don't** use abbreviations except for your middle name.
- **Don't** create a cramped and crowded look.
- **Don't** make statements you can't document.
- **Don't** use the passive voice.
- **Don't** change tense of verbs.
- **Don't** use lengthy sentences and descriptions.
- **Don't** refer to yourself as "I."
- **Don't** emphasize employment dates.
- **Don't** include negative information, such as your record.
- **Don't** include extraneous information (height, weight, marital status, age).
- **Don't** include salary information or references.

Resume "Do's"

- **Do** include an employer-centered objective.
- **Do** focus on your major accomplishments as they relate to employers' needs.

- **Do** include nouns so your resume can be scanned for keywords.
- **Do** use action verbs and the active voice to emphasize your accomplishments and keywords desired by employers.
- **Do** be direct, succinct, and expressive with your language.
- **Do** appear neat, well organized, and professional.
- **Do** use ample spacing and highlights (all caps, underlining, bulleting) for different emphases (except if it's an electronic resume).
- **Do** maintain an eye-pleasing balance.
- **Do** check carefully your spelling, grammar, and punctuation.
- **Do** clearly communicate your purpose and value to employers.
- **Do** communicate your strongest points first.
- **Do** keep your resume to one page but never more than two pages.

Resume Distribution

The only good resumes are the ones that get read, remembered, referred, and result in a job interview. Therefore, you must decide what to do with your resume. Are you planning to only respond to classified ads? Do you prefer posting your resume online with resume databases or e-mailing it to potential employers?

Most of your writing activities should focus on the hidden job market where jobs are neither announced nor listed. At the same time, you should respond to job listings in newspapers, magazines, human resources offices, and on websites, as well as get your resume into online resume databases. While this is largely a numbers game, you can increase your odds by the way you respond to the listings.

Most ads request a copy of your resume. Employers increasingly specify that it be sent by e-mail. You should respond with a cover letter and resume as soon as you see the ad. Depending on how much information about the position is revealed in the ad, your letter should be tailored to emphasize your qualifications as they relate to the ad. Examine the ad carefully. Underline any words or phrases which relate to your qualifications. In your cover letter, use similar terminology in emphasizing your qualifications. The most powerful cover letter you can write is the classic "T" letter (see page 92) which literally matches your skills and accomplishments with each of the employer's requirements.

Your best distribution strategy will be your own modification of the following:

- Selectively identify for whom you are interested in working.
- Send an approach letter.
- Follow up with a telephone call requesting an informational interview.

In more than 50 percent of the cases, you will get an interview. It is best not to include a copy of your resume with the approach letter. If you include a resume, you communicate the **wrong** message – that you want a job rather than information and advice. Chapter 11 outlines procedures for conducting this informational interview.

The Internet has quickly become the best friend of both employers and recruiters, who can recruit much faster and cheaper than through more traditional recruitment channels. Even small companies, now use the Internet to advertise jobs and search resume databases for qualified candidates. At the same time, the Internet offers job seekers an important tool to add to their job search arsenal. Make sure you include the Internet in your job search by posting your resume on numerous sites, conducting research, and networking for information, advice, and referrals. Start with the websites we listed on page 39.

Letter Power

Regardless of how you send your resume, it should be accompanied by a cover letter and follow the principles of good resume and business writing. Job hunting letters are like resumes – they advertise you for interviews. Like good advertisements, these letters should follow four basic principles for effectiveness:

1. Catch the reader's attention.
2. Persuade the reader of your benefits or value.
3. Convince the reader with evidence.
4. Move the reader to acquire the product – you!

In addition, the content of your letters should be the basis for conducting screening interviews as well as face-to-face interviews.

Basic Preparation Rules

Before you begin writing a job search letter, ask yourself several questions to clarify the content of your letter:

- What is the **purpose** of the letter?
- What are the **needs** of my audience?
- What **benefits** will my audience gain from me?
- What is a good opening sentence or paragraph for grabbing the **attention** of my audience?
- How can I maintain the **interest** of my audience?
- How can I best end the letter so that the audience will be **persuaded** to contact me?
- If sent with a resume, how can my letter best **advertise the resume**?
- Have I spent enough time **revising** and **proofreading** the letter?
- Does the letter represent my **best professional effort**?

Since your letters are a form of business communication, they should conform to the rules of good business correspondence:

- Organize what you will say by outlining the content of your letter.
- Know your purpose and structure your letter accordingly.
- Communicate your message in a logical and sequential manner.
- State your purpose immediately in the first sentence and paragraph.
- End by stating what your reader can expect next from you.
- Use short paragraphs and sentences; avoid complex sentences.
- Punctuate properly and use correct grammar and spelling.
- Use simple and straightforward language; avoid jargon or slang.
- Communicate your message as directly and briefly as possible.

The rules stress how to both **organize and communicate** your message. You should always have a specific purpose in mind as well as know the needs of your audience.

Types of Letters

Cover letters provide cover for your resume. You should avoid overwhelming a one-page resume with a two-page letter or repeating the contents of the resume in the letter. A short and succinct one-page letter with three paragraphs will suffice. The first paragraph should state your interests and purposes for writing. The second paragraph should highlight your possible value to the employer. The third paragraph should state that you will call the individual at a particular time to schedule an interview.

Approach letters are written for the purpose of developing job contacts, leads, or information as well as for organizing networks and getting interviews – the subjects of Chapter 10. Your primary purpose should be to get employers to engage in the 5R's of informational interviewing:

- **Reveal** useful information and advice.
- **Refer** you to others.
- **Read** your resume.
- **Revise** your resume.
- **Remember** you for future reference.

These letters help you gain access to the hidden job market by making important net-working contacts that lead to those all-important informational interviews.

Approach letters can be sent to many places to uncover job leads, or they can target particular individuals or organizations. It is best to target these letters since they have maximum impact when personalized in reference to a position.

The structure of approach letters is similar to that of other letters. The first paragraph states your purpose. You may want to open with a personal statement, such as *"John Taylor recommended that I write to you..."* or *"I am familiar with your..."* State your purpose, but do not suggest that you are asking for a job – only career advice or information. In your final paragraph, request a meeting and indicate you will call to schedule such a meeting at a mutually convenient time.

Thank-you letters may well become your most effective job search letters. They especially communicate your thoughtfulness. These letters come in different forms and are written for various occasions. The most common thank-you letter is written after receiving assistance, such as job search information and advice or a critique of your resume. Other occasions include:

- **Immediately after an interview**
- **Receive a job offer**
- **Rejected for a job**
- **Terminate employment**
- **Begin a new job**

The goal of the thank-you letter is to be **remembered** by potential employers in a **positive** light. In a job search, being remembered by employers is the closest thing to being invited to an interview and offered a job!

Exercises: Write your own resume, based on the principles and examples outlined in this chapter. Also, create four types of letters: "T", cover, approach, and thank-you relating to your resume and job search. Ask a thoughtful friend or professional to evaluate the quality of your resume and letters.

Functional Resume
(Limited Relevant Experience)

Gerald Walters

2713 Calder Avenue
Gary, Indiana 44432

Tel. 333-444-2222

Objective

An **entry-level warehouse position** with a small business that requires an energetic worker and values hard working, responsible, and loyal employees who are focused on getting the job done right and on time.

Summary of Qualifications

- Experienced in lifting heavy boxes and equipment
- Enjoy solving inventory problems and keeping a well organized work area
- Work well with supervisors, co-workers, and clients in getting jobs done
- Reputation for being a hard worker, quick learner, and adaptable

Experience

Heavy Lifting: Regularly handle heavy boxes and equipment weighing up to 100 pounds. Experienced in operating a forklift, packaging equipment, and computers.

Organization: Maintain a well-organized work area, keep good records, stock shelves, and load trucks. Sited by supervisor as one who is exceptionally dependable, well organized, and takes initiative in solving problems.

Customer Service: Experiencing in handling customer orders and solving customer problems.

Work History

State of Pennsylvania: Education and training programs centered on developing new workplace skills. Framington, Pennsylvania. 2004 to present.

Graysorn Construction Company: Varied maintenance jobs involving commercial construction and warehousing functions. Pittsburgh, Pennsylvania, 2002-2003.

Subway: Ordered supplies, maintained inventory, and provided good customer service. Pittsburgh, Pennsylvania, 2001.

Education/Training

- Currently completing GED
- Completed a basic workplace skills computer training course

Combination Resume
(Relevant Experience)

Victor Taylor
471 16th Street
Altanta, GA 33333
Tel. 222-333-4444

OBJECTIVE: A position as architectural drafter with a firm specializing in commercial construction where technical knowledge and practical experience will enhance construction design and improve building operations.

EXPERIENCE: <u>Draftsman</u>: A.C.T. Construction Company, Atlanta, GA. Helped develop construction plans for $15 million of residential and commercial construction. 2002-2004

<u>Cabinet Maker</u>: Garner-Williams Company, Birmingham, AL. Designed and constructed kitchen counter tops and cabinets; installed the material in homes; cut and laid linoleum flooring in apartment complexes. 1999-2000

<u>Carpenter's Assistant</u>: Thompson Associates, Atlanta, GA. Assisted carpenter in the reconstruction of a restaurant and in building of forms for pouring concrete. 1997-1998

<u>Materials Control Auditor</u>: Battles Machine and Foundry, Alanta, GA. Collected data on the amount of material being utilized daily in the operation of the foundry. Evaluated the information to determine the amount of materials being wasted. Submitted reports to production supervisor on the analysis of weekly and monthly production. 1993-1996

TRAINING: <u>Drafting School, Atlanta Vocational and Technical Center</u>, 2001. Completed 15 months of training in drafting night school.

EDUCATION: <u>Atlanta Community High School</u>, Atlanta, GA. Graduated in 1992.

PERSONAL: Single...willing to relocate...prefer working both indoors and outdoors...strive for perfection...hard worker...enjoy photography, landscaping, furniture design and construction.

REFERENCES: Available upon request.

"T" Letter
(Alternative to a Resume)

September 21, 20 __

Jack Tillman
ACE Electrical Solutions
2781 Washington Avenue
Baltimore, MD 17233

Dear Mr. Tillman:

I'm responding to your ad that appears in today's Baltimore Sun for an electrician. I believe I am an excellent candidate for this position. Given my interests, training, and experience as an electrician, I would bring to this position the following qualifications:

Your Requirements	My Qualifications
One year commercial experience	Completed one-year apprenticeship and served two years as an electrician's helper on complex commercial projects.
Responsible	Praised by previous employer and co-workers as being a quick starter who takes initiative, is responsible, and gets the job done well and on time.
Trouble-shooter	Skilled in solving complex wiring problems that have saved customers additional costs.
Good customer relations	Received several letters from repeat customers expressing satisfaction for quickly solving problems and proposing cost-effective solutions to lighting issues.

In addition, I know the importance of building strong long-term customer relations as part of building a small business. I enjoy taking on new challenges and working with teams to achieve company goals.

I believe there is a strong match between your needs and my qualifications. Could we meet soon to discuss how we might best work together? I'll call your office on Wednesday at 11am to see if your schedule might permit such a meeting.

I appreciate your consideration and look forward to speaking with you on Wednesday.

Sincerely,

Aaron Easton

Aaron Easton
eastonar@hotmail.com

Cover Letter
(Parts Manager)

7813 Peoria Avenue
Chicago, IL 60030

July 23, 20_____

Emily Southern
Atlas Auto Supply
153 West 19th Street
Chicago, IL 60033

Dear Ms. Southern:

Please accept the enclosed resume as my application in response to your ad in today's Chicago Tribune for a Parts Manager. You stated you needed an experienced manager who has worked with large equipment and who is familiar with ordering inventory and managing personnel.

I believe I have the necessary experience and skills to do this job well. During the past 10 years I have worked at all levels and in a variety of positions in the parts business. I began in receiving, moved on to manage a stockroom, took customer orders, and managed a parts warehouse with 11 employees. I'm experienced in operating computerized inventory systems. In my last job I decreased warehouse labor costs by 35% by installing a new inventory system.

I would appreciate the opportunity to interview for this position. Please expect a phone call from me on Thursday afternoon. I'll be calling for more information about the position as well as to answer any questions you may have about my candidacy.

Sincerely,

Terry Wilder

Terry Wilder
wildert@hotmail.com

Thank-You Letter
(Post Job Interview)

981 River Drive
Los Angeles, CA 13344

December 2, 20_____

Tom Peterson
Circulation Department
Los Angeles Gazette
2150 Waterfront Drive
Los Angeles, CA 13347

Dear Mr. Peterson:

I really appreciated having the opportunity to interview with you today for the position of Dispatcher. I remain extremely interested in this position since it is a perfect fit for my interests, skills, and experience. I am especially interested because it is an evening job. Since I am used to working an evening schedule, this would be a perfect schedule for me.

If I have not heard from you by next Friday, I will check back with you to see how your selection process is progressing. I look forward to hearing from you and hope I will have the opportunity to work with you.

Sincerely,

Steven Chase

Steven Chase
chasestev@yahoo.com

11

Network for Information, Advice, and Referrals

I F YOU LEARN ONLY ONE THING from this workbook, make sure it's networking. It's a powerful tool you should use throughout your work life. It's the ex-offender's best approach to quickly finding a job and dealing with the issue of disclosure.

The Secret to Getting Interviews and Job Offers

Everything you do up to this point in your job search should be aimed at **getting a job interview**. The most important secret in doing so is the **informational interview**, which yields useful job search information, advice, and referrals leading to job interviews and offers. Based on prospecting and networking techniques, these interviews minimize rejections and competition as well as quickly open the doors to employers. For ex-offenders, the informational interview is an ideal way to deal with a "criminal record."

If you want to quickly generate several interviews, you first need to understand how to initiate and use the informational interview. In so doing, you'll be exploring the **hidden job market** of unadvertised vacancies.

Learn to Effectively Prospect and Network

Research and experience clearly show the most effective means of communication are face-to-face and word-of-mouth. The informal, interpersonal system of communication is the central nervous system of the hidden job market. Appropriate methods for making important job contacts in this market are **prospecting and networking**. The best methods for getting these contacts to provide you with useful job information are **informational and referral interviews**.

Networking for information, advice, and referrals should play a central role in your overall job search. Remember, employers need to solve personnel problems. By conducting **informational interviews and networking**, you help employers identify their needs, limit their alternatives, and thus make decisions and save money. Especially for ex-offenders, such interviews and networking activities help relieve employers' anxiety about hiring what they might consider to be "risky" individuals.

At the same time, you gain several advantages by conducting these interviews:

- You are less likely to encounter rejections since you are not asking for a job – only information, advice, referrals, and to be remembered.
- You encounter little competition.
- You go directly to the people who have the power to hire.
- You are likely to be invited to job interviews based upon your referrals.

Since employers want to hire people they **like** both personally and professionally, you should communicate that you have the necessary personal **and** professional skills to perform the job. Prospecting, networking, and informational interviewing activities are the best methods for communicating such "qualifications" to employers.

Develop Networks

Networking is the process of purposefully developing relations with others. Networking in the job search involves connecting with other people who can help you find a job. Your network consists of you interacting with these other individuals. The more you develop, maintain, and expand your networks, the more successful should be your job search.

Your network is your interpersonal environment. While you may know and interact with hundreds of people, on a day-to-day basis you may encounter no more than 20 people. You frequently contact these people in face-to-face situations. Some people are more **important** to you than others. You **like** some more than others. And some will be more **helpful** to you in your job search than others. Your basic network may include friends, acquaintances, immediate family, distant relatives, spouse, supervisor, P.O., fellow workers, delivery service people, and local businesspeople and professionals, such as your banker, lawyer, doctor, minister, and insurance agent. You should contact many of these individuals for advice relating to your job search.

You need to **identify everyone in your network** who might help you with your job search. You first need to expand your basic network to include individuals you know and have interacted with over the past 10 or more years. Make a list of 100 or more people you know, such as:

- Relatives
- Your P.O.
- Former supervisors
- Teachers/instructors
- Ministers/clergy
- Church members
- Support group members
- Friends/pen pals
- Neighbors
- Former employers
- Social acquaintances
- Classmates
- Anyone you do business with:
  - store personnel
  - bank personnel
  - doctors
  - dentists
  - opticians
  - lawyers
  - real estate agents
  - insurance agents
  - travel agents
  - direct-sales personnel
- People you meet on the Internet

- Speakers at meetings you attend
- Delivery service personnel (Postal Service, UPS, Federal Express)

- Local leaders
- Politicians, including your local representative

You can probably think of many other people to put on your list. Try to identify those who have legitimate jobs and who are successful. In other words, you want to **run with real winners** who have good job-oriented contacts. Pretty soon you should have a long list of people to whom you can direct your networking activities.

Once you've developed your list of contacts, classify the names into different categories of individuals:

- Those in influential positions or who have hiring authority
- Those with job leads
- Those most likely to refer you to others
- Those with long-distance contacts

Select at least 25 names from your list for initiating your first round of contacts. You are now ready to begin an active prospecting and networking campaign which should lead to informational interviews, formal job interviews, and job offers.

After identifying your extended network, you should try to **link your network to the networks** of others. The figure on page 97 illustrates this linkage principle. Individuals in these other networks also have job information and contacts. Ask people in your basic network for referrals to individuals in **their** networks. This approach should greatly enlarge your basic job search network.

Develop a Prospecting Campaign for Information

The key to successful networking is an active and routine **prospecting campaign**. Salespersons in insurance, real estate, Amway, Shaklee, and other direct-sales businesses understand the importance of prospecting; indeed, many have turned the art of prospecting into a science as well as billion-dollar global businesses! The basic operating principle is **probability**: the number of sales you make is a direct function of the amount of effort you put into developing new contacts and following through. Expect no more than a 10 percent acceptance rate: for every 10 people you meet, nine will reject you and one will accept you. Therefore, the more people you contact, the more acceptances you will receive. If you want to be successful, you must collect many more "no's" than "yeses." In a 10 percent probability situation, you need to contact 100 people for 10 successes.

These prospecting principles are extremely useful for conducting a job search. Like sales situations, the job search is a highly ego-involved activity often characterized by numerous rejections accompanied by a few acceptances. While no one wants to be rejected, few people are willing and able to handle more than a few rejections. They take a "no" as a sign of personal failure – and quit prematurely. In fact, the typical job search looks something like this:

No, No, No, No, No, No, Maybe, No, No, No, Yes, No, No, No, No, No, No, No, Maybe, No, Maybe, Yes, No, No, No, No, Yes, Yes

Linking Your Networks to Others

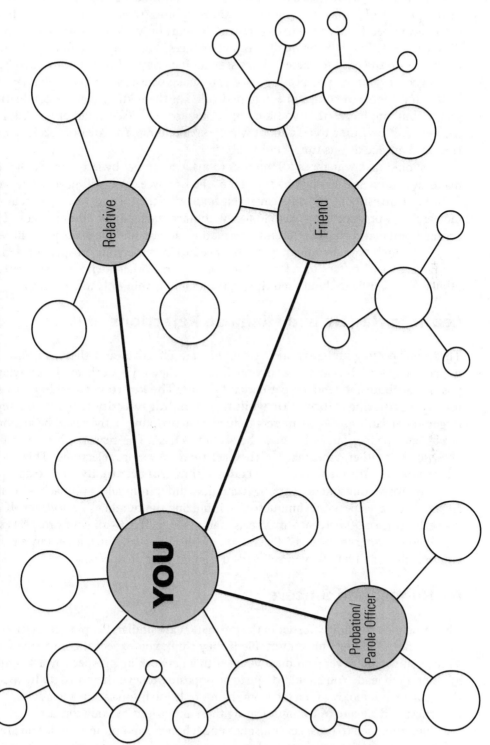

If you get disillusioned and quit after receiving four rejections, you will prematurely fail. While it may be initially hard to do, you need to continue making calls and writing letters in the process of "collecting" more rejections in order to get an acceptance. In fact, we often recommend that individuals get up in the morning with the idea of collecting at least 20 rejections! You will eventually get acceptances, but you must first deal with many rejections on the road to success. **Persistence does pay off in the long run.**

A good beginning prospecting pace is to make two new contacts each day. Start by contacting people in your immediate network. Let them know you are conducting a job search, but emphasize that you are only doing research (see Chapter 9). Ask for a few moments of their time to talk about what you are doing. You are only seeking **information and advice** at this time – not a job.

It should take you about 20 minutes to make a contact by letter or telephone. If you make two contacts each day, by the end of the first week you will have 10 new contacts for a total investment of less than seven hours. By the second week you may want to increase your prospecting pace to four new contacts each day or 20 each week. The more contacts you make, the more useful information, advice, and job leads you will receive. If your job search bogs down, you probably need to increase your prospecting activities.

Expect each contact to refer you to two or three others, who will also refer you to others. Your contacts should multiply considerably within only a few weeks.

Learn to Handle and Minimize Rejections

These prospecting and networking methods are effective, and they can have a major impact on your job search – and your life. But they only work for those who have a positive attitude and who are patient and persist. **The key to networking success is to focus on gathering information while also handling rejections.** Learn from rejections, forget them, and go on to more productive networking activities. The major reason direct-sales people fail is because they don't persist. The reason they don't persist is because they either can't take, or they get tired of taking, rejections. This should not happen to you. **Always welcome rejections: they will eventually lead to acceptances!**

Our prospecting and networking techniques differ from sales approaches in one major respect: we have special techniques for minimizing the number of rejections. If handled properly, at least 50 percent – maybe as many as 90 percent – of your prospects will turn into "yeses" rather than "nos." The reason for this unusually high acceptance rate is how you introduce and handle yourself as you contact your prospects.

Be Honest and Sincere

The principles of selling yourself in the job market are similar. People don't want to be put on the spot. They feel uncomfortable if they think you expect them to give you a job. Thus, you should never introduce yourself to a networking prospect by asking them for a job or a job lead. You should do just the opposite: relieve their anxiety by mentioning that you are not looking for a job from them – only job information and advice. You must be honest and sincere in communicating these intentions to your contact.

Your approach to prospects must be subtle, honest, and professional. You are seeking **information, advice, and referrals** relating to several subjects: job opportunities, your job search approach, your resume, and contacts who may have similar information, advice, and referrals. Most people gladly volunteer such information. They generally like to talk about themselves, their careers, and others.

This approach should yield a great deal of information, advice, and referrals from your prospects. One other important outcome should result from using this approach: people will **remember** you as the person who made them feel at ease and who received their valuable advice. If they hear of job opportunities for someone with your qualifications, chances are they will pass the information on to you. After contacting 100 prospects, you will have created 100 sets of eyes and ears to help you in your job search!

Practice the 5R's of Informational Interviewing

The guiding principle behind prospecting, networking, and informational interviews is this: **The best way to get a job is to ask for job information, advice, and referrals; never ask for a job**. Remember, you want your prospects to engage in the 5R's of informational interviewing:

- **Reveal** useful information and advice.
- **Refer** you to others.
- **Read** your resume.
- **Revise** your resume.
- **Remember** you for future reference.

If you network according to this principle, you should join the ranks of thousands of successful job seekers who have experienced the 5R's of informational interviewing. Largely avoiding the advertised job market, you may find your perfect job through such powerful networking activities.

Approach Key People

Whom should you contact within an organization for an informational interview? Contact people who are **busy**, who have the **power to hire**, and who are **knowledgeable** about the organization. The least likely candidate will be someone in the human resources department. Most often the heads of operating units are the most busy, powerful, and knowledgeable individuals in the organization. However, getting access to such individuals may be difficult. Some people at the top may appear to be informed and powerful, but they may lack information on the day-to-day personnel changes or their influence is limited in the hiring

We recommend contacting several types of people. Aim for the busy, powerful, and informed, but be prepared to settle for less. Secretaries, receptionists, and the person you want to meet may refer you to others. From a practical standpoint, you may have to take whomever you can schedule an appointment with. Sometimes people who are less powerful can be helpful. Talk to a secretary or receptionist sometime about their boss or working in the organization. You may be surprised by what you learn!

Conduct the Interview, Including the "CR" Question

An informational interview will be relatively unstructured compared to a formal job interview. Since you want the individual to advise you, make sure you ask questions that will give you useful information. You, in effect, become the interviewer. You should structure this interview with a particular sequence of questions. Most questions should be open-ended, requiring the individual to give specific answers.

The structure and dialogue for the informational interview might go something like this. You plan to take no more than 45 minutes for this interview. The first three to five minutes will be devoted to small talk – the weather, traffic, the office, mutual acquaintances, or an interesting or humorous observation. Since these are the most critical moments in the interview, be especially careful how you communicate nonverbally. Begin your interview by stating your appreciation for the individual's time. Use your own words, but follow the "gist" of the statement below:

"I want to thank you again for scheduling this meeting with me. I know you're busy. I appreciate the special arrangements you made to see me on a subject which is very important to my future."

Your next comment should reiterate your purpose as stated in your letter:

"As you know, I am exploring job and career alternatives. I know what I do well and what I want to do. But before I commit myself to a new job, I need to know more about various career options. I thought you would be able to provide me with some insights into career opportunities, job requirements, and possible problems or promising directions in the field of _____."

A statement of this type normally will get a positive reaction from the individual who may want to know more about what it is you want to do. Be sure to clearly communicate your job objective. If you can't, you may indicate that you are lost, indecisive, or uncertain about yourself. The person may feel you are wasting his or her time.

Your next line of questioning should focus on "how" and "what" questions centering on (1) specific jobs and (2) the job search process. Begin by asking about various aspects of specific jobs:

- Duties and responsibilities
- Knowledge, skills, and abilities required
- Work environment relating to employees, work, deadlines, stress
- Advantages and disadvantages
- Advancement opportunities and outlook
- Salary ranges

Your informer will probably take a great deal of time talking about his or her experience in each area. Be a good listener, but make sure you move along with the questions.

Your next line of questioning should focus on your job search activities. You need as much information as possible on how to:

- Acquire the necessary skills
- Best find a job in this field
- Overcome any objections employers may have to you
- Uncover job vacancies which may be advertised
- Develop job leads
- Approach prospective employers

Your next line of questioning should raise the "CR" question – your criminal record. This is a good time to disclose what may be a red flag for many employers. The question might be something like this, but it must honestly reflect your situation in the most positive way:

> *"I have a potential problem that I would appreciate your advice on. I'm currently on parole. A few years ago, when I was running with the wrong crowd, I did some very stupid things related to drugs. As a result, I spent two years in Paris State Prison. I lost everything – family, friends, and my self-esteem. While I hit bottom, I swore I would turn my life around. In fact, being incarcerated was the best thing to happen to me at that stage in my life. It was a real wake-up call. I got my GED, took a couple of college courses, participated in vocational training programs, and have excellent references from my supervisor, caseworker, and parole officer. I now know what I want to do with my life. However, when employers learn about my criminal record, they may automatically reject me. If you were in my situation, how would you handle the criminal record issue with employers?"*

The advice you get in response to this question may be some of the most important advice you get as you network. Indeed, you may discover many people in your network may try to bend over backwards to help you reenter the workforce despite your criminal record. This is an excellent time to fully disclose your key red flag issue. Again, remember you're not interviewing for a job – just getting valuable information and advice. The advice will help you overcome any reluctance to reveal your background to employers with whom you will be interviewing for an actual job.

Your final line of questioning should focus on your resume. Do not show your resume until you pose this last set of questions. The purposes of these questions are to: (1) get the individual to read your resume in-depth, (2) acquire useful advice on how to strengthen it, (3) be referred to prospective employers, and (4) be remembered. With the resume in front of you and the other person, ask the following questions:

- Is this an appropriate type of resume for the jobs I have outlined?

- If an employer received this resume in the mail, how do you think he or she would react to it?

- Do you see possible weaknesses or areas that need to be improved?

- What about the length, paper quality and color, layout, and type style/size? Are they appropriate?

- What should I do with this resume? Broadcast it to hundreds of employers with a cover letter? Use a "T" letter instead?

- How might I best improve the form and content of my resume?

- Who might be most interested in receiving this resume?

You should obtain useful advice on how to strengthen both the content and use of your resume. Most important, these questions force the individual to **read** your resume, which, in turn, may be **remembered** for future reference.

Your last question is especially important in this interview. You want to be both **remembered** and **referred**. Some variation of the following question should help:

> *"I really appreciate all this advice. It is very helpful and it should improve my job search considerably. Could I ask you one more favor? Do you know two or three other people who might be willing to assist me with these same questions? I want to conduct as much research as possible, and their advice might be helpful also."*

Before you leave, mention one more important item:

> *"During the next few months, if you hear of any job opportunities for someone with my interests and qualifications, I would appreciate being kept in mind. And please feel free to pass my name on to others."*

Send a nice thank-you letter – preferably by mail – within 48 hours of completing this informational interview. Express your genuine gratitude for the individual's time and advice. Restate your interests, and ask to be remembered and referred.

Be sure to follow up on any useful advice you receive, particularly referrals. Approach referrals in the same manner you approached the person who gave you the referral. Write a letter requesting a meeting. Begin the letter by mentioning:

> *"Mr./Ms. _____ suggested that I contact you concerning my research on careers in _____."*

If you continue prospecting, networking, and conducting informational interviews, soon you will be busy conducting interviews and receiving job offers. While 100 informational interviews over a two-month period should lead to several formal job interviews and offers, the pay-offs are uncertain because job vacancies are unpredictable. We know cases where the first referral turned into a formal interview and job offer. More typical cases require constant prospecting, networking, and informational interviewing activities. The telephone call or letter inviting you to a job interview can come at any time. While the timing may be unpredictable, your persistent job search activities will be largely responsible for the final outcome.

12

Develop Winning Job Interview Skills

WHILE THE JOB INTERVIEW IS the most important job search activity, it also is the most stressful job search experience. Your application, resume, and letters may get you to the interview, but you must perform well in person in order to get a job offer. Knowing the stakes are high, most people face interviews with dry throats and sweaty palms; it is a time of great stress. You will be on stage, and you need to be well prepared.

Unlike the informational interview (pages 99-103), where you asked most of the questions, in the job interview you will primarily respond to questions from the employer.

A Two-Way Communication Exchange

An interview is a two-way communication exchange between an interviewer and interviewee. It involves both verbal and nonverbal communication. While we tend to concentrate on the content of what we say, research shows that approximately 65 percent of all communication is **nonverbal**. Furthermore, we tend to give more **credibility** to nonverbal than to verbal messages. Regardless of what you say, how you dress, sit, stand, use your hands, move your head and eyes, and listen communicates either positive and negative messages.

Job interviews have different purposes and can be negative in many ways. From your perspective, the purpose of an initial job interview is to get a second interview or a job offer, and the purpose of the second interview is to get more interviews until a job offer is forthcoming. However, for many employers, the purpose of the interview is to eliminate you from additional interviews or a job offer. The interviewer wants to know why he or she should **not** hire you. The interviewer tries to do this by identifying your weaknesses. These differing purposes can create an adversarial relationship and contribute to the overall interviewing stress experienced by both the applicant and the interviewer.

Since the interviewer has certain expectations about required personalities and performance in candidates, he or she wants to **identify your weaknesses**. You must counter by **communicating your strengths** to lessen the interviewer's fears of hiring you. Recognizing that you are an unknown quantity to the employer, you must raise the interviewer's expectations of you.

Avoid 42 Common Interview Errors

Employers report encountering many job seekers who make a variety of interview errors that quickly knock them out of competition. Make sure you don't make any of these mistakes, which constitute a handy list of interview "don'ts":

1. Arrives late to the interview.
2. Comes to the interview with a friend, relative, or child.
3. Makes a bad impression – rude and obnoxious – in the waiting area.
4. Dresses inappropriately and looks sloppy and unkempt.
5. Wears sunglasses, blue jeans, and heavy-duty boots.
6. Presents a poor appearance and negative image.
7. Expresses negative attitudes, often saying *"can't"* or *"didn't."*
8. Offers lots of excuses and blames others for weaknesses or problems.
9. Engages in inappropriate behavior – shows off tattoos and leg injury.
10. Appears somewhat incoherent and unfocused.
11. Uses poor grammar and seems inarticulate.
12. Gives short and incomplete answers to questions.
13. Lacks a sense of direction or purpose.
14. Appears ill or has a possible undisclosed medical condition.
15. Volunteers personal information that would be illegal to ask.
16. Emits bad body odors.
17. Shows little enthusiasm, drive, or initiative.
18. Lacks confidence and self-esteem.
19. Appears too eager and hungry for the job.
20. Communicates dishonesty or deception.
21. Seems too smooth and superficial.
22. Appears evasive when asked about possible red flags.
23. Speaks negatively of previous employers and co-workers.
24. Maintains poor eye contact and fidgets a lot.
25. Offers a limp or overly firm handshake.
26. Shows little interest in the company.
27. Talks about salary and benefits early in the interview.
28. Is discourteous, ill-mannered, and disrespectful – argues a lot.
29. Tries to look cool and speaks an inappropriate street language.
30. Tells inappropriate jokes and laughs a lot.
31. Talks too much – a real motor-mouth.
32. Drops names to impress the interviewer.
33. Appears needy and greedy.
34. Fails to talk about accomplishments.
35. Does not ask questions about the job or employer.
36. Appears self-centered rather than employer-centered.
37. Demonstrates poor listening skills.
38. Seems not bright enough for the job.
39. Fails to know his/her worth when talking about compensation.
40. Forgets to bring appropriate documents, including a list of references.

41. Closes the interview by just getting up and leaving.
42. Never follows up.

Observe 43 Interview "Do's"

There are certain things you need to know and do before, during, and after the job interview. Each phase of the interview has its own separate set of "do's":

Preparing for the Interview

1. **DO** prepare your wardrobe, questions, and answers before the day of the interview.
2. **DO** research the company/organization, the job, and comparable salaries and benefits (see Chapter 9).
3. **DO** plan to sell yourself throughout the interview, from the moment you enter the door to 24 hours after the interview.
4. **DO** ask a friend or relative to help you prepare for the interview by role playing the interviewer and you, the interviewee.
5. **DO** practice giving positive employer-centered answers to possible interview questions, but never memorize answers that will make you sound rehearsed, appear insincere, and contribute to nervousness, especially when you forget your "lines."
6. **DO** prepare to address some really tough questions about your background, especially why the interviewer should hire someone with a criminal record, your work and educational achievements, your goals, and whether or not you are bonded.
7. **DO** look at yourself in the mirror and listen to what you say and how you say it, and then grade yourself and your performance from 1 to 10. Keep doing this until you become a "10." If you can't grade yourself, find someone who is a tough and objective evaluator.
8. **DO** outline a 30-second pitch of why you should be hired that you can occasionally repeat in different ways during the interview.
9. **DO** develop five one- to two-minute stories giving good examples of your major strengths and accomplishments that support your job objective.
10. **DO** learn how long it will take to get to the interview location, plan your transportation, and then plan to arrive at least 20 minutes early.
11. **DO** gather any documents you need to take to the interview, such as a list of references, a mock application form, your resume, drivers license, Social Security number, examples of your work, and any letters of recommendation or commendation.
12. **DO** ask people you plan to use as references if you may use them as references in your job search.
13. **DO** lower your stress level and nervousness by preparing well, taking deep breaths, and focusing on the interviewer rather than yourself.
14. **DO** write down any questions you need to ask the interviewer.
15. **DO** tell yourself that this is going to be the best day for starting your new life.
16. **DO** check the weather before you leave, just in case you need an umbrella or coat.
17. **DO** get a good night's sleep, avoid alcohol, and eat lightly the day before the interview.
18. **DO** practice good personal hygiene, from bathing and brushing teeth to washing hair, shaving, and cleaning hands and fingernails.

Arriving At the Interview Site

19. **DO** arrive on time.
20. **DO** come alone – no friends, relatives, or children should enter the building with you.
21. **DO** remove your coat before sitting down in the waiting area.
22. **DO** observe the surroundings and visit the restroom.
23. **DO** be courteous, professional, sincere, open, and honest at all times and with everyone you meet, including those in the waiting area before the actual interview; everyone you meet may be "interviewing" you and thus could be important to the final hiring decision.
24. **DO** behave yourself properly in the waiting room by being seen doing something relevant to the job or company, such a reading a company brochure, or asking thoughtful company-related questions (not salary).

Greeting the Interviewer

25. **DO** stand up and greet the interviewer by looking him or her in the eye, extending your hand, giving a firm handshake, and stating your first and last name: *"Hi, I'm John Strong."*
26. **DO** address the interviewer by his or her proper title and last name: Mr./Mrs./Miss/Dr. _____. No first names unless asked to do so by the interviewer or people you meet.
27. **DO** wait to be seated before sitting down in the interviewer's office.
28. **DO** engage in some small talk, perhaps about the weather, something interesting you see in the office (painting, book, sculpture, diploma).

Conducting the Formal Interview

29. **DO** bring a pen and notebook to take notes during the interview.
30. **DO** sit up straight with a slightly forward lean, relax, keep your hands to your side or on your lap, listen carefully, project yourself, focus on the interviewer rather than on yourself, and look alive and happy.
31. **DO** appear friendly, enthusiastic, energetic, interested, and alert throughout the interview.
32. **DO** control your emotions, avoid being defensive, keep your cool, and go on to do your best, even if the interviewer asks you an illegal or insulting question
33. **DO** recover quickly from any errors you make. If you stumble or knock something over, or know you gave a bad answer to a question, keep on moving. Excuse yourself, go on to the next question, and focus on other more important things rather than try to keep recovering from a mistake. How you recover may be more important to the interviewer than the error you made.
34. **DO** speak well of others and situations, even though you may have had problems in the past. Always think of something good to say about other people and situations you have been in. How you talk about them is a good indicator of your attitudes, motivations, and behavior. Take, for example, how you might respond to questions concerning your incarceration or being fired. Put an honest, but positive, spin on such experiences.
35. **DO** give complete 30-second to two-minute answers to questions that constantly focus on your goals and strengths.
36. **DO** ask thoughtful questions about the job, company, employer, and competition, which you should have listed and written on a card or in your notebook. Refer to your notes to make sure you ask the right questions and impress upon the interviewer that you are prepared and interested in the company.

37. **DO** let the interviewer finish his or her questions or comments before responding.
38. **DO** delay any discussion of salary and benefits until the very end of the interview and after you have received a job offer. Prematurely talking about salary and benefits can quickly kill your candidacy as well as put you at a disadvantage.

Closing the Interview

39. **DO** let the interviewer initiate the close of the interview by indicating it's time to move on.
40. **DO** ask for a business card so you can follow up with a nice thank-you letter.
41. **DO** close the interview properly by (1) summarizing what you understand to be the responsibilities of the job, (2) stating why you believe this job would be an excellent fit for both you and the employer, (3) expressing your gratitude for the opportunity to interview for the position, (4) asking when the interviewer plans to make the hiring decision and when you might hear again from the interviewer, and (5) asking if it would be okay if you call the interviewer in a few days to check on the status of your candidacy.

Following Up the Interview

42. **DO** follow up with a nice thank-you letter within 24 hours.
43. **DO** make the follow-up call you indicated you would make.

Prepare to Answer Questions

You should practice the actual interview by mentally addressing questions interviewers are likely to ask. Most of these questions will relate to your educational background, work experience, career goals, personality, and related concerns. Start with *"Tell me about yourself,"* which we addressed on pages 12-13. Other frequently asked questions include:

Education

- Describe your educational background.
- Why did you drop out of school?
- What was your grade point average?
- Why were your grades so low? So high?
- What subjects did you enjoy the most? The least? Why?
- What leadership positions did you hold?
- Did you do the best you could in school? If not, why not?
- What educational programs did you participate in while in prison?
- Are you planning to go to college?
- What will you major in?
- If you could, what would you change about your education?
- What type of specialized training have you received?

Work Experience

- What were your major achievements in each of your past jobs?
- Why did you change jobs before?
- What is/was your typical workday like?
- What did you like about your boss? Dislike?

- If I called your last supervisor and asked about you, what might he tell me concerning your work habits and accomplishments?
- Which job did you enjoy the most? Why? Which job did you enjoy the least? Why?
- Have you ever been fired? Why?
- What did you especially like about your last job?
- Do you think you have enough experience for this job?

Career Goals

- Why do you want to join our company?
- Why do you think you are qualified for this position?
- Why are you looking for a job?
- What ideally would you like to do?
- Why should we hire you?
- How would you improve our operations?
- What do you want to be doing five years from now?
- How much do you expect to be making five years from now?
- What are your short-range and long-range career goals?
- If you were free to choose your job and employer, where would you go?
- What other types of jobs are you considering? Companies?
- When will you be ready to begin work?
- How do you feel about relocating, traveling, working overtime, working shifts, and working on weekends?
- What attracted you to us?

Personality and Other Concerns

- Tell me about yourself.
- What are your major weaknesses? Your major strengths?
- What causes you to lose your temper?
- What do you do in your spare time? Any hobbies?
- What types of books do you read?
- What role does your family play in your career?
- How well do you work under pressure? In meeting deadlines?
- How much initiative do you take?
- What types of people do you prefer working with?
- How _____ (creative, analytical, tactful, etc.) are you?
- If you could change your life, what would you do differently?

While different employers will ask different combinations of questions, we recommend spending extra time preparing for these seven most frequently asked questions:

- Tell me about yourself.
- Why should I hire you?
- What are your major weaknesses?
- Tell me about your plans for the future.
- How do your most recent jobs relate to this position?
- How would your previous employers characterize you?
- What are your salary requirements?

Give Positive Answers

Your answers to employers' questions should be positive and emphasize your **strengths**. The interviewer wants to know what's wrong with you – your **weaknesses**. When answering questions, both the **substance** and **form** of your answers should be positive. For example, such words as "couldn't," "can't," "won't," and "don't" may create a negative tone and distract from the positive and enthusiastic image you are trying to create. While you cannot eliminate all negative words, at least recognize that the type of words you use makes a difference; try to better manage your word choice. Compare your reactions to the following answers:

QUESTION: **Why do you want to work here?**

ANSWER 1:   *I just got out of prison and need a job. I don't know if you'll give me the job since I haven't worked in a few years. But I won't give you any trouble. I think I'll like working here. The people seem nice. I hope you won't hold my record against me.*

ANSWER 2:   *I've always wanted to work for this company. You have a great reputation for being a leader in commercial moving and having the most professional movers in the business. My experience as a truck driver, my recent training in customer service, and my strong organization and communication skills are ideally suited for this position. I'm really excited about joining your team and making sure that you continue being the very best in this business. I also have some ideas on how we might be able to save money on two of the regular delivery routes. I am ready to take on more responsibilities and hope to work closely with you.*

Which one has the greatest impact in terms of projecting positives and strengths? The first answer communicates too many negatives and makes the interviewee sound like a beggar. The second answer is positive and upbeat in its emphasis on skills, accomplishments, and the future.

In addition to choosing positive words, select **content information** which is positive and **adds** to the interviewer's knowledge about you. Avoid simplistic "yes/no" answers; they say nothing about you. Instead, provide information which explains your reasons and motivations behind specific events or activities. For example, how do you react to these two factual answers?

QUESTION: **I see you recently completed your GED. Did you drop out of high school?**

ANSWER 1:   *Yes, I did.*

ANSWER 2:   *Yes. I did very poorly in high school – bad grades along with a poor attitude and attendance. I flunked two grades and was often suspended for bad behavior. I even attended an alternative school and got into more trouble, ending up in the juvenile detention center for two years. There I meet a wonderful teacher, Mrs. Taylor, who took a personal interest in me. She urged me to study for my GED. I really hadn't read until I met her. With her encouragement, I studied real hard and scored a 60 on the GED. Getting my GED really got me focused on planning my future, which now centers on more education and training. I know I can do whatever I set my* *mind to do. I really love working with numbers. As you can see from my resume, I've taken a couple of accounting courses at T. L. Johnson Junior College. I'm planning to complete my A.A degree within the next three years. I'm hoping this bookkeeping position will eventually lead to an accounting position within your company. I'm really excited about this position and have enjoyed meeting your staff and learning about your work.*

Let's try another question reflecting possible objections to hiring you:

QUESTION: **Your background bothers me. Why should I hire someone with a criminal record?**

ANSWER 1:   *I can understand that.*

ANSWER 2:   *I understand your hesitation in hiring someone with my background. I would, too, if I were you. Yes, many people who get out of prison go back to their old ways and soon return to prison. But I'm not like others who may play games to get the job and then disappoint you. I've been there and learned more than you can imagine. I was young, foolish, and made a terrible mistake. But I decided to turn my attitude and life around. Prison was actually good for me. I took advantage of every educational, vocational training, and work opportunity available while I was incarcerated. I now have clear goals, which include working for someone like you. I also have excellent character, education, and work references from several people I've worked with over the past two years, including my parole officer who knows my case very well. If you have any doubts about my character and ability to do this job, I would urge you to put me on a lengthy probationary period during which time you can be assured that you made the best hiring decision. Frankly, I plan to become your star performer within the first three months.*

The first answer is incomplete. It misses an important opportunity to give evidence that you have resolved this issue in a positive manner, which is clearly reflected in the second response.

All of these examples stress the basic point about effective interviewing. Your single best strategy for managing the interview is to **emphasize your strengths and positives and be enthusiastic about the job**. Questions come in several forms. Anticipate these questions, especially the negative ones, and practice the "gist" of positive responses in order to project your best self in an interview situation.

Deal With the Incarceration Question

The question you probably dread most relates to your incarceration. How do you respond to it in the most positive manner? How should you handle it? Should you raise the issue if the employer does not? Questions about your criminal record are on the employer's mind whether they are spoken or unspoken. Are you going to repeat your negative behavior? Have you really changed, or are your problems likely to recur and affect your work on your next job?

Even if the employer does not ask about your incarceration, you may decide to bring it up yourself either because you are required to do so, or because you don't want to worry about someone else telling him in the future. You want to explain the situation honestly, but in the most positive way that you can. It is important that you address each of the red

> **Exercise:** On eight separate sheets of paper, write answers to these eight questions (one question per sheet):
>
> 1. Why should I hire you?
> 2. Why should I hire someone with a criminal record?
> 3. Tell me about yourself.
> 4. What are your weaknesses?
> 5. Tell me about your plans for the future.
> 6. How do your most recent jobs relate to this position?
> 7. How would your previous employers characterize you?
> 8. What are your salary requirements?

flags in your background as honestly **and** in as positive a light as possible. Making excuses or blaming others for your problems will not reassure the employer that he will not inherit similar problems with your behavior if he hires you! You could respond to the incarceration question **or** you might bring it up yourself with something like the following:

You know about my incarceration. I would like to explain the situation and the changes I have made in my life to make sure it never happens again.

You immediately want to stress two important points:

1. You accept that your behavior was wrong. You are aware of the negative consequences of the behavior that got you into trouble.

2. You take responsibility for the past inappropriate behavior and don't put the blame on others.

Don't talk too much about these first two points. Many ex-offenders talk too long and in too much detail about their past crime(s). Accept responsibility, but don't dwell on it! Move on. You want to talk more about the two areas – those that deal with the changes you have made for your future:

3. Mention the changes you have made in your life so this will not happen again. The situation that supported the past negative behavior no longer exists. For example, if part of the problem in the past was that you got in with the wrong crowd and their activities influenced your behavior, demonstrate that your present situation is different. You no longer hang out with that crowd. You now associate with a different group of people who do not get into trouble.

4. As you have changed your situation, you have made it easier for you to change your behavior. You have overcome the negative cycle.

5. It was a difficult learning experience you had to go through. But you have "done your time" and are ready to get on with a more positive life. You want the chance to demonstrate to the employer that with your skills and your attitude you will make a positive contribution to the company.

Anticipate Behavior-Based Questions

More and more employers are conducting "behavior-based interviews." These interviews are specific and challenge candidates to provide concrete examples of their achievements. Such interviews are designed to uncover **clear patterns of behavior** which are good predictors of future performance. Behavior-based questions are likely to begin with some variation of:

- *Give me an example of a time when you . . .*
- *Give me an example of how you . . .*
- *Tell me about how you . . .*

Depending on the position in question, you may or may not encounter these types of questions. Behavior-based questions especially arise during interviews for positions involving decisions of responsibility. If you are asked such questions, give examples of your relevant accomplishments. Briefly describe the situation, enthusiastically explain what you did, and indicate the outcome. For example, if the interviewer asks,

"Tell me about a time when you anticipated a potential problem."

The applicant might respond,

"When I was working at McDonald's, I noticed the children's playground was unprotected from the parking area. I told my supervisor that this could be a dangerous situation if someone accidentally jumped the curb and plowed into a crowd of kids. He took a look at the area and agreed that heavy-duty guard rails needed to be installed in front of the curb. It was a good thing he did this. Three weeks after they were installed, a lady got into her car, mistakenly put it in drive, and slammed into the guard rail. It really scared a group of 30 kids and parents who were there for a birthday party. Had we not installed the guard rail, I'm afraid several of the kids would have been injured or even killed. I really felt good about doing this. I also was glad someone at work listened to me and took appropriate action. My supervisor promoted me after that incident."

Obviously you want to select examples that promote your skills and have a positive outcome. Even if the interviewer asks about a time when something negative happened, try to select an example where you were able to turn the situation around and something positive came out of it. For example, if asked, *"Tell me about a time you made a bad decision,"* try to identify an occasion where:

- Even though it wasn't the best decision, you were able to pull something positive out of the situation.

- Though it was a poor decision, you learned from it, and in the next similar situation you made a good decision or know how you will handle it differently the next time a similar situation arises.

- It was a bad decision but the negative outcome had only minor impact.

In other words, try to pull something positive – either that you did or that you learned – out of even a negative experience you are asked to relate. As you prepare for your interview, consider situations where you:

- demonstrated leadership
- solved a problem
- increased company profits
- made a good/poor decision

- handled changing events
- handled criticism
- met a deadline/missed a deadline
- worked as part of a team

Add to this list other behavioral questions you think of that pertain to the job for which you are applying.

Exercise: On seven separate sheets of paper, write stories that relate to these seven behavior-based questions (one question/story per sheet):

1. Tell me about a time in which you failed to meet a deadline.
2. Give me an example of how you took initiative in solving a problem.
3. Tell me how you took responsibility for a problem you created.
4. Give me examples of your three most satisfying accomplishments in your last job.
5. Tell me about a time in which you were fired from a job.
6. Give me an example of how you worked effectively under pressure.
7. Tell me how you saved your boss money.

You may encounter hypothetical questions in which you are asked not what you did, but what you would do if something occurred. With hypothetical questions, the interviewer is less interested in your actual answer – often there is no correct or incorrect response – than in your thought process. He or she wants to know how you would solve a problem or respond to a particular type of situation.

Face Situational Interviews

More and more employers also are conducting situational interviews, which enable them to observe the actual behavior of candidates in particular situations. Again, you may or may not encounter such interviews. While candidates can prepare for behavior-based interviews by focusing on their accomplishments and telling stories about their past performance, such interviews are still primarily verbal exchanges.

Situational interviews rely less on analyzing verbal cues and more on analyzing actual observed behavior or performance in key work-related situations. The popular television program _The Apprentice_ is a good example of situational interviews. Employers especially like conducting these interviews, because they know candidates can't prepare well for the situations in which they may be asked to perform. These interviews give employers a chance to observe a candidate's decision-making skills in the process of solving work-related problems. Many of these interviews involve mock scenarios in which a candidate is asked to role play. For example, someone interviewing for a customer service position may be asked to play the role of a customer service representative by handling telephone calls from irate customers. In this scenario the interviewer has a chance to observe the candidate in action. Does he or she talk down, get angry, or resolve the problem to the satisfaction of the customer? The behavior of a competent customer service representative can be readily observed in such a role playing scenario. Other examples of situational interviews may involve mock negotiation sessions, selling a product, constructing something, or repairing a product.

Ask Thoughtful Questions

Interviewers expect candidates to ask intelligent questions concerning the organization and the nature of the work. In fact, many employers indicate that it's often the quality of the questions asked by the candidate that is instrumental in offering them the job. Moreover, you need information and should indicate your interest in the employer by asking questions. Consider asking some of these questions if they haven't been answered early in the interview:

- Tell me about the duties and responsibilities of this job.
- What's the most important thing I should know about your company?
- How does this position relate to other positions within this company?
- How long has this position been in the organization?
- What would be the ideal type of person for this position? Skills? Personality? Working style? Background?
- Can you tell me about the people who have been in this position before? Backgrounds? Promotions? Terminations?
- Whom would I be working with in this position?
- Tell me something about these people. Their strengths? Their weaknesses? Their performance expectations?
- What am I expected to accomplish during the first year?
- How will I be evaluated?
- Are promotions and raises tied to performance criteria?
- Tell me how this operates?
- What is the normal salary range for such a position?
- Based on your experience, what type of problems would someone new in this position likely encounter?
- I'm interested in your career with this organization. When did you start? What are your plans for the future?
- How do people get promoted and advance in this company?
- What does the future look like for this company?
- Could I meet with the person who will be my supervisor?

You may want to write your questions on a 3x5 card and take them with you to the interview. While it is best to recall these questions, you may need to refer to your list when the interviewer asks you if you have any questions. You might do this by saying: *"Yes, I jotted down a few questions which I want to make sure I ask you before leaving."*

13

Negotiate Salary and Benefits Like a Pro

T HE QUESTION OF WAGES/SALARY may be raised anytime during the job search. Employers may want you to state a salary expectation figure on an application form, in a cover letter, or over the telephone. Most frequently, however, employers will ask about salary during the employment interview.

Depending on the level of the position and the type of job you seek, the following discussion may or may not be relevant to you. The greater the job responsibilities, the more flexibility you and the employer have to negotiate wages/salary and benefits.

Timing Is Everything

If at all possible, keep the wage/salary question **open** until the very last. Revealing your hand early in the interview will not be to your advantage. Even with application forms, cover letters, and telephone screening interviews, try to delay the discussion of money by stating "open" or "negotiable." After all, the ultimate purpose of your job search activities is to demonstrate your **value** to employers. You should not attempt to translate your value into dollar figures until you have had a chance to convince the employer of your worth. This is best done near the end of the job interview, preferably after you have received a job offer.

Let the employer initiate the salary question. And when he or she does, take your time. Don't appear too anxious. While you may know – based on your previous research – approximately what the employer will offer, try to get the employer to state a figure first. If you do this, you will be in a stronger negotiating position.

Reach Common Ground and Agreement

After finding out what the employer is prepared to offer, you have several choices. First, you can indicate that his or her figure is acceptable to you and thus conclude your final interview. Second, you can haggle for more money in the hope of reaching a compromise.

Third, you can delay final action by asking for more time to consider the figure. Finally, you can tell the employer the figure is unacceptable and leave.

The first and the last options indicate you are either too eager or playing hard-to-get. We recommend the second and third options. If you decide to reach agreement on salary in this interview, negotiate in a professional manner. You can do this best by establishing a **salary range** from which to bargain in relation to the employer's salary range. For example, if the employer indicates that he or she is prepared to offer $35,000 to $40,000 (or $9.50 to $10.50 per hour), you should establish common ground for negotiation by placing your salary or wage range into the employer's range. Your response to the employer's stated range might be:

> *"Yes, that does come near what I was expecting. I was thinking more in terms of $40,000 to $45,000 (or $10.50 to $11.50 per hour)."*

You, in effect, place the top of the employer's range into the bottom of your range. At this point you may be able to negotiate a salary of $40,000 to $45,000 (or a wage rate of $10.50 to $11.50 per hour), depending on how much flexibility the employer has with money. Many employers have more flexibility than they admit. Wages for entry-level positions and individuals with little related experience will have less room for negotiation.

Once you have placed your expectations at the top of the employer's salary range, you need to emphasize your value with **supports,** such as examples, illustrations, descriptions, definitions, statistics, comparisons, or testimonials. It is not enough to simply state you were "thinking" in a certain range; you must state why you believe you are worth the salary you want. Using statistics and comparisons, you might say, for example:

> *"The salary surveys I have read indicate that for the position of _____ in this industry and region the salary is between $40,000 and $45,000. Since, as we have discussed, I have extensive experience in all the areas you outlined, I would not need training in the job duties themselves – just a brief orientation to the operating procedures you use here at _____. I'm sure I could be up and running in this job within a week or two. Taking everything into consideration – especially my skills and experience and what I see as my future contributions here – I really believe a salary of $45,000 is fair compensation. Is this possible here at _____?"*

Another option is to ask the employer for time to think about the salary offer. You want to consider it for a day or two. A common professional courtesy is to give you at least 48 hours to consider an offer. During this time, you may want to carefully examine the job. Is it worth what you are being offered? Can you do better? What are other employers offering for comparable positions? If one or two other employers are considering you for a job, let this employer know his or her job is not the only one under consideration. This should give you a better bargaining position. Contact the other employers and let them know you have a job offer and that you would like to have your application status with them clarified before you make any decisions with the other employer. Depending on how much flexibility an employer may have to accelerate a hiring decision, you may be able to go back to the first employer with another job offer. With a second job offer in hand, you should greatly enhance your bargaining position.

In both recommended options, you need to keep in mind that you should always negotiate from a position of knowledge and strength – not because of need or greed. Learn about salaries for your occupation, establish your value based on your skills and work experience, discover what the employer is willing to pay, and negotiate in a professional manner. For how you negotiate your salary will affect your future relations with the employer. In general, applicants who negotiate well will be treated well on the job.

Useful Salary Negotiation Resources

For more information on salary negotiations for both job seekers and employees, see our *Salary Negotiation Tips for Professionals*, *Dynamite Salary Negotiations*, and *Get a Raise in 7 Days* (Impact Publications). These books outline various steps for calculating your worth and conducting face-to-face negotiations, including numerous sample dialogues. For online assistance with salary information and negotiations, be sure to visit these websites:

- Salary.com   www.salary.com
- JobStar   www.jobstar.org
- Monster.com   http://salary.monster.com
- SalaryExpert   www.salaryexpert.com
- Quintessential Careers www.quintcareers.com/salary_negotiation.html
- Riley Guide   www.rileyguide.com/netintv.html
- Robert Half International www.rhii.com

Checklist of Compensation Options

When it's time to talk about compensation with an employer, it's always a good idea to prepare a written statement of your current, or previous, compensation package. This statement should summarize the various elements included in your compensation package as well as the value of each. Some elements, such as an office with a window, may not have a dollar value but they may be important to you.

One of the easiest ways to survey your compensation options and assign value to your ideal compensation package is to use the following checklist of compensation options. Consider each item and then value it with a dollar amount. While some of the items may not be relevant to your situation, many will. When finished, add up the total dollars assigned to get a complete picture of the value of your present or past compensation package. You can later compare this to future offers.

Element	Value
Basic Compensation Issues	
Base salary	$ _____
Commissions	$ _____
Personal performance bonuses/incentives	$ _____
Cost of living adjustment	$ _____
Overtime	$ _____
Health Benefits	
Medical insurance	$ _____
Dental insurance	$ _____
Vision insurance	$ _____
Prescription package	$ _____

- Life insurance $ _____
- Accidental death and disability insurance $ _____

Vacation and Time Issues

- Vacation time $ _____
- Sick days $ _____
- Personal time $ _____
- Holidays $ _____
- Flextime $ _____
- Family leave $ _____

Retirement-Oriented Benefits

- Defined-benefit plan $ _____
- 401(k) plan $ _____
- Deferred compensation $ _____
- Savings plans $ _____
- Stock-purchase plans $ _____
- Stock options $ _____

Education

- Professional continuing education $ _____
- Tuition reimbursement for you or family members $ _____

Perquisites

- Cellular phone $ _____
- Company car or vehicle/mileage allowance $ _____
- Child care $ _____
- Cafeteria privileges $ _____
- Personal use of frequent-flyer awards $ _____
- Convention participation: professionally related $ _____
- Parking $ _____
- Athletic club memberships $ _____
- Use of company-owned facilities $ _____
- Office with a window $ _____
- Laptop computers $ _____
- Employee discounts $ _____
- Incentive trips $ _____
- Discounted buying club memberships $ _____

Home Office Options

- Personal computer $ _____
- Internet access $ _____
- Copier $ _____
- Printer $ _____
- Separate phone line $ _____
- Separate fax line $ _____
- Incidental/support office functions $ _____
- Office supplies $ _____
- Furniture and accessories $ _____

TOTAL $ _____

14

Develop an Action Plan for Making It On the Outside

Y
OU MUST TAKE SPECIFIC ACTIONS to effectively implement this book. Re-entry is hard work and involves many psychological ups and downs attendant with unrealistic expectations, missed opportunities, and frequent disappointments. You often face the possibility of being **rejected**. And this is precisely the major barrier you will encounter to effective implementation. For many people are unwilling to take more than a few rejections.

Turn Rejections Into New Opportunities

Planning is the easiest part of any task. Turning plans into reality is the most difficult challenge. It's relatively simple to set goals and outline a course of action divorced from the reality of actually doing it. But if you don't take action, you won't get expected results.

Once you take action, be prepared for rejections. Employers will tell you *"Thank you – we'll call you,"* but they never do. Other employers will tell you *"We have no positions available at this time for someone with your qualifications"* or *"You don't have the qualifications necessary for this position."* Whatever the story, you may face many disappointments on the road to success.

Don't assume you are rejected because of your background. As we noted on page 96, rejections are a normal part of finding employment and getting ahead. Rejections should be important learning experiences which help you better understand yourself, employers, and the job-finding process. More important, you will likely be rejected many times before you will be accepted. Expect, for example, 10 rejections or "no's" for every "maybe" or "yes" you receive. If you quit after five or eight rejections, you prematurely end your job search. If you **persist** in collecting two to five more "no's," you will likely receive a "yes." Most people quit prematurely, because their egos are not prepared for more rejections. Therefore, you should welcome rejections as necessary for getting to a "yes."

Get Motivated and Work Hard

Assuming you have a firm understanding of the 10 steps and how to relate them to your goals, what do you do next? The next steps involve **motivation and hard work.** Just how motivated are you to seek a new job or career and thus change your life? Our experience is that individuals need to be sufficiently **motivated** to make the first move and do it properly.

If you go about your job search half-heartedly – you just want to "test the waters" to see what's out there – don't expect to be successful. You must be committed to achieving specific goals. Make the decision to properly develop and implement your job search and be prepared to work hard in achieving your goals.

Find Time to Take the Necessary Actions

Once you've convinced yourself to take the necessary steps to find a job, you need to find the **time** to properly implement your job search according to the 10 steps outlined on page 3. This requires setting aside specific blocks of time for identifying your motivated abilities and skills, developing your resume, writing letters, making telephone calls, and conducting the necessary research and networking required for success. This whole process takes time. If, for example, you can set aside two hours each day to devote to your job search, you will spend 14 hours a week or 56 hours a month on your search. However, you should and can find more time than this for these activities.

Time and again we find successful job hunters routinize specific job search activities. They make contact after contact, conduct numerous informational interviews, submit many applications and resumes, and keep repeating these activities in spite of encountering rejections. They learn that success is just a few more "no's" and informational interviews away. They face each day with a positive attitude fit for someone desiring to turn their life around – I must collect my 10 "no's" today because each "no" brings me closer to a "yes"!

Commit Yourself in Writing

You may find it useful to commit yourself in writing to achieving job search success. This is a very effective way to get both motivated and directed for action. Start by completing the job search contract on page 121 and keep it near you.

In addition, you should complete weekly performance reports to yourself. These reports identify what you actually accomplished rather than what your good intentions tell you to do. Make copies of the performance and planning report form on page 122 and use one each week to track your actual progress and to plan your activities for the next week.

If you fail to meet these written commitments, issue yourself a revised and updated contract. But if you do this three or more times, we strongly suggest you stop kidding yourself about your commitment and motivation to find a job. You need a better structure for implementation. Start over again, but this time find someone who can assist you with your job search – a trusted friend, a career professional, or a support group that will make sure you complete all job search tasks on time. Such individuals and groups can be the missing ingredient for keeping you focused and making sure you get the expected results that come with following each of the 10 steps outlined in this book.

Job Search Contract

1. I'm committed to changing my life by finding the right job for me. Today's date is _____.

2. I will effectively manage my time so that I can successfully complete my job search and find a high quality job. I will begin by spending at least two hours each day in completing the 10 steps to re-entry and job search success outlined on page 3.

3. I will begin my job search on this date: _____.

4. I will involve _____ with my job search.   (specific individuals/groups)

5. I will spend at least one week conducting research on different jobs, employers, and organizations. I will begin this research during the week of _____.

6. I will complete my skills identification (Step 4) by _____.

7. I will complete my objective statement (Step 5) by _____.

8. I will complete my resume (Step 7) by _____.

9. Each week I will:

   - make _____ new job contacts.

   - conduct _____ informational interviews.

   - follow up on _____ referrals.

10. I understand the importance of rejections and how to best handle them as outlined on pages 96 and 119.

11. My first job interview will take place during the week of _____.

12. I will begin my new job by _____.

13. I will make a habit of learning one new skill each year.

         Signature: _____

         Date: _____

Weekly Job Performance and Planning Report

1. The week of: _____.

2. This week I:

   - wrote ____ job search letters.
   - sent ____ resumes and ____ letters to potential employers.
   - completed ____ applications.
   - made ____ job search telephone calls.
   - completed ____ hours of job research.
   - set up ____ appointments for informational interviews.
   - conducted ____ informational interviews.
   - received ____ invitations to a job interview.
   - followed up on ____ contacts and ____ referrals.

3. Next week I will:

   - write ____ job search letters.
   - send ____ resumes and ____ letters to potential employers.
   - complete ____ applications.
   - make ____ job search telephone calls.
   - complete ____ hours of job research.
   - set up ____ appointments for informational interviews.
   - conduct ____ informational interviews.
   - follow up on ____ contacts and ____ referrals.

4. Summary of progress this week in reference to my Job Search Contract commitments:

   _____

   _____

   _____

   _____

   _____

   _____

   _____

   _____

   _____

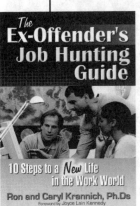

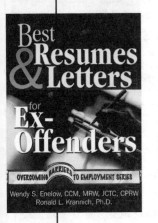